PLEASE SAY YES

SHORT PLAYS ABOUT PROMPOSING

---

by Nicole B. Adkins, Will Coleman, Anne G'Fellers-Mason, Megan Gogerty, Neeley Gossett, Adam Hahn, Laura King, Samantha Macher, Wendy-Marie Martin and Ricky Young-Howze

Collection curated by Nicole B. Adkins

www.youthplays.com
info@youthplays.com
424-703-5315

LIST OF PLAYS

If At First You Don't Succeed by Wendy-Marie Martin

Game On by Neeley Gossett

Forming Bonds by Ricky Young-Howze

The Water Tower by Will Coleman

Ante Up by Laura King

Hashtag Adorable by Samantha Macher

One Last Trick by Anne G'Fellers-Mason

Banned from Student Activities by Adam Hahn

Prom Ninja by Nicole B. Adkins

The Clarinet Section is Sick of Your Garbage by Megan Gogerty

PRODUCTION NOTES

The plays can be performed as individual pieces or grouped together in any combination to create a show of the desired length and performed under the title *Please Say Yes: Short Plays About Promposing.*

There are 7-34+ possible roles in the collection. If each were single cast, there are roles for 17 females, 11 males, and 6 of either gender (or more chorus members in *Hashtag Adorable*). The collection could be produced with as few as 4 females and 3 males, with each actor playing multiple roles.

ACKNOWLEDGMENTS

A staged reading was produced by Elm Street Cultural Arts Center on December 12, 2015. Special thanks to Siobhan

Brumbelow, Education Director at Elm Street Cultural Arts Center, for casting and organizing this event.

The reading was directed by Nicole B. Adkins with the following cast: Jonah Bowling, Brandon Cali, Hailey Elswick, Jenna Klein, Beth Leak, Cole Lindner, Nicole Miller, Carson Newsome, MJ Smith, Isabelle Vinelli, Kristina Welch and Michaela White.

IF AT FIRST YOU DON'T SUCCEED

A short comedy by
Wendy-Marie Martin

CAST OF CHARACTERS

JOSH, a high school junior with a crush on Adelia.

GREG, a high school junior and Josh's best friend.

SHANNON, Greg's girlfriend and Josh's self-appointed promposal consultant.

ADELIA, a shy Latina high school sophomore with intense allergies.

MANNY, Adelia's protective older brother.

PRODUCTION NOTES

// is a signifier for the next line of dialogue to begin.

All dual dialogue is meant to take place simultaneously.

Adelia's speech after her tongue swells does not need to be understandable at all. In fact, the less we understand, the better.

(Lights up on JOSH, GREG and SHANNON hanging out in the quad before school.)

SHANNON: You'd better hurry or someone's going to beat you to it —

JOSH: I know —

GREG: The man knows, babe —

SHANNON: Well if he knows why doesn't he DO something?

JOSH: I can't think of anything special enough for her —

SHANNON: Greg didn't get all stressed out about it. // He just said —

GREG: Yeah, I was all "Wanna?"

SHANNON: —and I said "Sure, why not." Done —

GREG: Learn from the master, my friend.

JOSH: Yeah but you guys are practically married. Besides, you're a Neanderthal —

SHANNON: Truth! You can tell by   **GREG:** Hey —
his elongated skull and supraorbital
ridge...and broad, projecting nose.

JOSH: Right?

GREG: Sitting right here guys.

JOSH: Sorry, dude. Just saying I need a different strategy. I've never even said two words to her —

SHANNON: Oh my god, I know...pigeons!

JOSH: Pigeons?

SHANNON: Yeah, you know, those ones that fly messages around. Just aim it at her math class —

JOSH: A promposal pigeon? Seriously?

GREG: Lame —

SHANNON: Fine then. Just…send her a note or something —

GREG: Or flowers. Ladies love the blossom.

SHANNON: How would you know?

GREG: Read it on the interwebs —

SHANNON: You don't have time to wait, Josh. Just…go ask her.

JOSH: I can't just ask. You know that. I need something…special.

(Greg starts digging in the trash can.)

SHANNON: Gross. What are you doing?

GREG: Uh…saving the day? Here, man. Use these. *(Pulling bedraggled roses out of the trash:)* Clearly the last guy doesn't need them.

JOSH: Dude, you're a genius —

SHANNON: Seriously? They're covered in bad promposal energy. I can feel the failure from here —

GREG: Don't blame the blossom, woman. Maybe our friend Josh here can reverse the curse…

(ADELIA enters with her brother MANNY.)

Or suffer the same fate as the last guy.

SHANNON: That's her older brother, Manny —

JOSH: Just what I need, an overprotective brother.

SHANNON: He's harmless.

(The bell rings.)

Ask her. *(To Greg:)* Come on, Einstein. First period starts in five minutes.

GREG: You've got this, man. Reverse the curse!

(*Shannon drags Greg off. Josh tries to hide as Adelia and Manny walk closer.*)

MANNY: Out of the question. You know Papa wouldn't approve.

ADELIA: But I already asked Mama and she said I could —

MANNY: You go, I go —

ADELIA: Manny —   **MANNY:** That's the deal. They ask
                            you, they're asking me, too.

ADELIA: Fine. Then find a date, 'cause I'm going this year.

MANNY: *If* someone asks you.

(*Josh approaches with the flowers.*)

ADELIA: Well, maybe *I'll* — (*Sneeze.*) —ask *them* —

(*Adelia sneezes a few times in succession. Josh is just about to ask when Manny notices him, grabs the flowers and throws them.*)

MANNY: Stay away from my sister with those, man. You could kill her —

JOSH: Kill...? I —   **ADELIA:**   (*Sneezing:*)   That's...
                              (*Sneeze.*) Not true. I —

JOSH: Oh my god, I'm so sorry. I didn't. I...oh man —

(*Josh runs off.*)

MANNY: Idiot. Don't people realize flowers can kill?

(*Adelia is still having a sneeze attack.*)

Come on, we gotta get you away from those. Papa will kill us both if you end up in the hospital again.

(Manny and Adelia exit. A bell rings. Josh, Greg and Shannon enter with lunch bags.)

SHANNON: Allergic?

JOSH: Totally allergic. He said I could have killed her —

SHANNON: Shut. Up.   **GREG:** That's intense.

SHANNON: Allergic to flowers. How sad.

JOSH: I have to think of something else.

GREG: I know, dude. Cook for her. The ladies love it when you cook for them —

SHANNON: How would you know?

GREG: Saw it on the interwebs —

JOSH: Wait. How 'bout... *(Josh pulls out a brownie wrapped in cellophane.)* Left over from my mom's Bunco party last night.

GREG: Your mom's killer brownies? Dude, I've actually dreamt about those —

JOSH: I know, right? Secret family recipe —

SHANNON: That's perfect. Give her the brownie.

GREG: Oh man —

JOSH: I can't just give her a brownie with no explanation —

SHANNON: Write a note and give it to her. Trust me.

(Adelia and Manny enter, walking toward them. Adelia's nose is red and she holds a handful of tissues. She takes a hit off her inhaler. Bell rings.)

GREG: Better hurry, dude. Opportunity awaits.

(Greg and Shannon exit. Josh throws the brownie back into his lunch bag in a panic and looks for a pencil.)

JOSH: Damn it.

MANNY: I'll kick that guy's ass if you want me to—

ADELIA: I'm fine. It's just allergies. Stop pretending you're all tough, // Manuel—

MANNY: Pretending?

ADELIA: Besides, I think he's sweet—

MANNY: You don't even know who he was going to ask. What if they were for someone else?

ADELIA: What if they weren't?

(As they approach, Josh holds out his lunch bag.)

MANNY: What do you want—

JOSH: Oh...I, uh...sorry I...here.

(He tosses the bag to Manny and runs off.)

ADELIA: I told you! Give it to me—

MANNY: He handed it to me—   **ADELIA:** Give it!

(Adelia grabs the bag, looks for a note, then pulls out the brownie and takes a bite.)

ADELIA: Hmm...delicious... *(Beat.)* ...wait...what...?

MANNY: Adi what's wrong?

ADELIA: Pep...pepp—

(She shoves the brownie at Manny. He inspects.)

MANNY: Peppers? Who puts red peppers in a brownie?

ADELIA: *(As if her tongue is swelling:)* My tongue—

MANNY: Come on, let's get you to the nurse's office.

(Adelia and Manny exit as the sixth period bell rings, signifying the end of the school day. Greg, Shannon and Josh enter.)

GREG: Dude, that's harsh. She had to go to the hospital?

JOSH: That's what Susan Blackwell told me. I feel awful.

SHANNON: I told you in the first place to just ask her—

GREG: Yeah, preferably before you kill her.

JOSH: Very funny. I hope she's okay.

(Adelia enters alone. Her nose is still bright red and her tongue is now swollen, making it hard to understand her.)

SHANNON: There she is—

GREG: Hospital at lunch and back for sixth period? She's a survivor, dude. Respect. *(Beat.)* Where's the bodyguard?

JOSH: I don't see—

SHANNON: She's alone. Perfect. Go ask her.

JOSH: But—

GREG: Ask her, dude.   **SHANNON:** Now!

JOSH: But—

GREG: Ask.   **SHANNON:** ASK HER.

(Shannon and Greg push him toward Adelia.)

JOSH: Adelia. Wait.

(Josh catches up to Adelia, but she's cautious.)

I'm clean. Nothing. I swear. Unless you're allergic to me.

(She relaxes and gives him a little smile.)

I am so sorry I didn't know... I mean... I just wanted to...I mean...do...do you...

(Awkward pause. Deep breath and...)

ADELIA: Do you wanna go   **JOSH:** Do you wanna prom
to prom?   to the go with me?

No no...you first.   Wait, what?

JOSH: Adelia...will you be my prom date?

ADELIA: I would love to go to the prom with you.

JOSH: Was that a yes?

ADELIA: Yes, yes, YES!!!

(Awkward hug. Manny enters as Adelia sneezes.)

MANNY: There you are. *(To Josh:)* You. Step away from my sister.

(Josh puts his hands up and steps away. Manny pulls out a lint roller and rolls Josh's sweatshirt.)

Is that cat hair?

JOSH: Cats, too?

MANNY: Cats, flowers, bell peppers, leather —

JOSH: Leather?

MANNY: Leather. I said leather, didn't I? Latex, bee stings, peanuts, pollen, dust mites —

ADELIA: Stop —

JOSH: It's cool. I get it. He's just trying to protect you. *(To Manny:)* Look, just...get me a list. I'll keep her safe. Deal?

(Josh extends his hand to shake. Manny looks from his sister to Josh and back. Long beat.)

MANNY: Fine. Deal.

(They shake hands.)

Looks like I'd better find a date, eh?

(Josh hands his sweatshirt to Manny, then he offers his hand to Adelia, who takes it and continues to sneeze as they walk past Greg and Shannon.)

GREG: Success. I had no doubts, my friend.

(End of play.)

The Author Speaks

What inspired you to write this play?
I was looking for an unusual conflict within the promposal concept that wasn't the usual boy wants girl, girl's not interested type thing. It happened to be allergy season when I wrote it, so I chose to explore ways in which an extremely allergic character could build conflict throughout the play and still lead to the happy ending. I specifically researched a mix of expected and unexpected allergies and played with the various side effects of each before choosing flowers, red bell peppers and cat hair as the main allergies in the play. The allergies Manny lists at the end are all legitimate, though.

Was the structure or other elements of the play influenced by any other work?
The play is structured after a normal high school bell schedule. They meet before school, at lunch and after school with the bell as a sign of the passing of time. The overprotective brother and cross-cultural romance were influenced a bit by the relationships in *West Side Story.* Although there is not tension about the fact that Adelia is Latina and Josh clearly isn't, the cultural differences do influence how they deal with each other.

Have you dealt with the same theme in other works that you have written?
This is the first time I've written Latino characters. Having a layer of cultural differences creates a foundation of challenge for Josh. As we learn of Adelia's father's strict nature and meet her brother, Manny, it's clear that Josh has his work cut out for him before he even starts to set off some serious allergic reactions. However, the fact that Manny approves of Josh as an acceptable date for his sister shows that there's no tension in regards to mixing cultures in the end.

What writers have had the most profound effect on your style?
For this play, I feel like the screenwriters of *Bill & Ted's Excellent Adventure*, Chris Matheson and Ed Solomon, were in my brain. The combination of the confident but dumb best friend and quirky string of failed attempts by Josh remind me of the playful and silly nature of this movie.

What do you hope to achieve with this work?
I hope this play will make high school audiences laugh up until the "aww" moment when Josh and Adelia end up together. I also wanted to create roles specifically for Latino actors and show a cross-cultural romance that isn't about culture clash while still respecting that the characters come from different backgrounds. I also hope my play gives anyone afraid to ask that special someone to the prom the courage to try. After all, it can't get worse than putting your potential date in the hospital with red pepper, right?

What were the biggest challenges involved in the writing of this play?
I spent a lot of time researching allergies and trying to choose the right ones with the best side effects to add to the humor and dramatic tension. There are so many allergies out there! Trying to keep a balance between taking the allergic reactions seriously and finding the most humor in them was difficult. I also wrote Latino characters for the first time and wanted to do so with respect and authenticity. It's very important to me that all of my characters have real intentions and backgrounds that feed their dialogue.

What are the most common mistakes that occur in productions of your work?
I tend to write with a quick tempo, both in dialogue and in scene changes. But often my plays are produced with pauses, slow fadeouts and overly long changes due to an attempt to

overcomplicate them. The transitions are meant to be simple and quick, as is most of the dialogue. Also, I use // as a signifier for the next line of dialogue to begin and dual dialogue, which is meant to take place simultaneously. However, often I realize that the director/actors may not fully understand this formatting. That's why I've started clarifying these two tools in my production notes.

What inspired you to become a playwright?
My high school drama teacher was a playwright and made us write our own monologues and scenes in acting class, so playwriting was a natural extension of theatre making for me. I started as an actor and then moved into directing and at one point realized that playwriting is the culmination of everything I love to do. Playwriting allows me to act all the roles and direct the scenes in my mind as I write without ever having to get on stage.

How did you research the subject?
I did quite a bit of research on allergies for this play, actually. I learned of some lesser-known allergies. A leather allergy, for example, was news to me. If you get a poison ivy-type rash on your feet after wearing leather shoes, you could be allergic to chemicals used in the leather tanning process. I'd never thought of that before. Also, some people are allergic to swimming in water. The allergy is called aquagenic urticarial and doctors have no idea why people who have it get hives from water. Luckily, antihistamines help relieve the discomfort. I discovered a bunch of unusual allergies during my research, like an allergy to exercise, electricity, coins, cold and even to touch. With such a short play, though, I had to choose allergies that would move the dramatic action forward while creating as much humor as possible at the same time. I also learned about the varying levels of severity as far as the allergic reactions go and which ones would cause discomfort

as opposed to those that could be fatal if not treated immediately.

Are any characters modeled after real life or historical figures?
Although not consciously, I do feel like the role of Greg is based on characters found in the *Bill & Ted* movies. He's got that surfer philosopher energy and manages to be poetic even when he says totally ridiculous things. He also takes himself very seriously, no matter how silly his words.

What is your writing process?
My writing process varies. Often with longer works, I start with an outline and character sketches and flesh the action out from there. This play began with the characters of Josh and Adelia, and as I strove to build more conflict, Adelia's brother appeared. Then, Greg and Shannon popped in to add some comic relief to the play. I knew there had to be an attempt at a promposal and that I wanted it to end with success, but that was about it at the start. I am very lucky to have written this piece during a class taught by Nicole B. Adkins, who curated this collection, at Hollins University. The dramaturgical input from Nicole and my classmates through the process really helped to make the play stronger and tighter.

Shakespeare gave advice to the players in *Hamlet*; if you could give advice to your cast what would it be?
Make extreme choices without losing the tempo of the piece. No matter how bold your character choices may be, though, remember these are authentic people with specific intentions and varied tactic palettes. Don't always go for the first choice. Play around and try different acting choices before landing on who you think your character is and what they may or may not do. Most importantly, have fun.

About the Author

Wendy-Marie Martin earned her MFA in Playwriting from the Playwright's Lab at Hollins University and holds a BFA in Acting as well. She's written, directed and produced intimate theatre projects in the U.S. and Europe. Her short plays have been produced in Germany, the Netherlands, Australia, and the U.S. She is also creator and Executive Producer of The Red Eye 10s Play Festival, an international festival of original shorts. Wendy-Marie is a member of the Dramatists Guild, TCG and the Playwrights' Center, and a former resident playwright at SkyPilot Theatre Company in Los Angeles and Tesseract Theatre Company in St. Louis.

GAME ON

A short drama by
Neeley Gossett

CAST OF CHARACTERS

CARLY, female, a high school soccer player.

MARA, female, a high school soccer player.

BRETT, male, a high school soccer player.

(*CARLY, a star high school soccer player, and her friend MARA, also a soccer player, finish writing "Prom?" all over a soccer ball.*)

CARLY: I feel like this is so cheesy.

MARA: It's so *not* cheesy. It's romantic.

CARLY: We just wrote "prom" with a question mark all over a soccer ball. Mara, it reeks of cheese.

MARA: It's the perfect promposal. You both play soccer. What's better than using a soccer ball to prompose?

CARLY: You know how I feel. I want him to prompose to me. Not the other way around.

MARA: Come on, Carly. You're getting weak on me. We're the ones who never fall for that traditional, girly BS. You're the toughest goalie I know, girl or guy. Start acting like it.

CARLY: I don't know if I can do it.

MARA: Look at it this way. You can't back out now. It would be a waste of a soccer ball.

CARLY: We can still use it to kick around.

MARA: And every time you kick it, you'll remember how you could have gone to prom with Brett, but you were too afraid to ask him.

CARLY: I'm boyish enough as it is. I don't need to ask anyone to prom. It may cause my testosterone to shoot up so high that I grow chest hair.

MARA: Just don't wear a low-cut dress.

CARLY: Would you stop?

MARA: God. Sensitive.

CARLY: Sorry. I'm just nervous.

MARA: It's fine. Don't worry about it. Girls ask guys all the time.

CARLY: Name someone we know who asked a guy.

MARA: *(Beat.)* I'm sure there's someone.

CARLY: See. It's only me. I'm the only one asking a guy to prom.

MARA: If you want to reach your goals, you've got to go after them.

CARLY: You sound like that horrible motivational speaker we had during advisement last week.

MARA: Look, I have it on good authority that Brett's not going with anyone else. He's gonna say "yes." If nothing else, he wouldn't miss the chance to do the worm on the dance floor.

CARLY: That was the fifth grade.

(Brett enters.)

Look. There he is.

MARA: You got this?

CARLY: I guess. It's now or never.

MARA: Good luck, chica.

(Mara exits. Carly and Brett are left alone on stage.)

CARLY: Hey, Brett.

(Carly kicks the ball to Brett. Brett kicks it back. Carly kicks it to him again. He kicks it back to her. She kicks it to him.)

CARLY: Read it.

BRETT: It says prom.

CARLY: It does.

BRETT: Is this one of those —

CARLY: I know it's stupid.

BRETT: I've seen the videos.

CARLY: Yeah?

BRETT: Mostly flash mobs.

CARLY: I was gonna do that.

BRETT: You were?

CARLY: I'm kidding.

BRETT: I'm glad.

CARLY: So. The ball says prom. *(Beat.)* And it has a question mark.

BRETT: Look — I don't know, Carly — I —

CARLY: Friends. I want to go as friends. Just friends.

BRETT: I hate to say it, but I kinda had someone else in mind.

CARLY: Oh, okay. Don't worry about it.

BRETT: Really?

CARLY: Really. I understand if you don't want to go.

BRETT: Thanks. You know, you're one of the coolest girls I know.

CARLY: Thanks?

BRETT: No, really. You are.

CARLY: Can you tell me who it is? Who you're going to ask?

BRETT: I'm not sure.

CARLY: But you said you had someone in mind.

BRETT: Well, yeah. A few people. I was thinking about asking Madison. The one who sang at the assembly.

CARLY: She's going with Raphael.

BRETT: Oh, then I'll ask Madison with the sexy glasses.

CARLY: She's going with Dan.

BRETT: Football Dan?

CARLY: No, Lacrosse Dan.

BRETT: Then Madison in our chem lab.

CARLY: She's going with Chad.

BRETT: With the weird eyes?

CARLY: That's Brad.

BRETT: Then who's Chad?

CARLY: Redhead.

BRETT: Swim team?

CARLY: Dive team, but yeah, that's him.

BRETT: She's going with someone on the dive team?

CARLY: What's wrong with the dive team?

BRETT: Speedos. That's what's wrong.

(A few beats pass as the rejection becomes real for Carly. Disappointment sets in.)

CARLY: So, you don't have anyone to take?

BRETT: I'll find someone.

CARLY: No. No. I'm sure you will.

BRETT: I didn't mean—I just don't I want to waste senior prom on someone I don't like. I mean someone who's just my friend.

CARLY: *(Pushing back tears:)* I get it.

BRETT: You should ask someone you really like. Don't waste a promposal on me.

CARLY: Okay. *(Beat.)* I will.

BRETT: You'll have more fun that way. I mean—it's supposed to be the best night of your life.

CARLY: God, I hope not.

BRETT: I mean, who knows? We've had a great soccer season. And if I bring a hot girl to prom—I go out on top. You know what I'm saying?

CARLY: I don't think I do.

BRETT: I've got to make the most of this month. You'll never have as much fun as an adult as you do in high school.

CARLY: High school's fine, but I don't think my life's going to end in a few weeks.

BRETT: I hear my friends say it all the time. They're all like, "Life sucks after high school."

CARLY: Are those your twenty-year-old friends who come back to hang out in the school cafeteria during lunch?

BRETT: It's the cheapest lunch in town.

CARLY: They could order from a fast food dollar menu like everyone else.

BRETT: It's not that easy.

CARLY: *(Beat.)* I'm playing up north in the fall.

BRETT: I know. That's gonna suck. You won't have any of your friends there with you.

CARLY: I think I'll be okay.

BRETT: Let's keep up with each other. Maybe I'll see you back here at a football game in the fall?

CARLY: I'll probably have practice, or something else to do.

BRETT: Then text me sometime next year, okay?

CARLY: I'll try.

(He tosses the ball to her and exits.)

(She waits until he's gone and then sinks to the ground. She puts her head in her hands. Mara enters and Carly stands. She bushes herself off and pretends that nothing has happened.)

MARA: So, how'd it go?

CARLY: He said no.

MARA: Don't joke like that.

(Mara sees Carly's face.)

Oh, my God. What happened?

CARLY: He wants to go with a hot girl.

MARA: He said that?

CARLY: Yep.

MARA: I'm so sorry.

CARLY: He wants to go with someone hot because it's going to be the best night of his life.

MARA: Wow. Poor guy.

(Mara and Carly start to giggle a bit.)

Well, Carly, if this is the best night of his life, let him have it. It's only downhill for him from here. You can come back from college and see him hanging out with the other townies at the diner by the highway.

CARLY: *(Laughing:)* I've got something to ask you.

(Carly kicks Mara the soccer ball.)

Prom?

MARA: With you?

CARLY: Why not?

MARA: I'd be honored.

CARLY: We could ask the rest of the team. Stacy's the only one with a date.

MARA: We wouldn't want them to miss out on the best night of their life.

CARLY: That would be a tragedy.

MARA: We could make an entrance wearing jerseys over our dresses.

CARLY: Could we rethink that?

MARA: Maybe. But we might as well go all out. It's downhill from here anyway.

CARLY: Right. I almost forgot.

(Carly kicks the ball offstage. They exit.)

The Author Speaks

What inspired you to write this play?
In high school, I was never asked to a dance. However, I ended up going to four homecomings and two proms. Even though no one invited me, I refused to stay home. Why should the lack of a boy's promposal dictate whether or not I had a good time? I brought my super handsome guy friends from other schools. Several of them obviously had no interest in me (or any girls). There were no goodnight kisses, but there was great dancing, and they looked dapper in photos. Ultimately, I was inspired to write a play about a girl who overcomes rejection and refuses to stay home.

Was the structure or other elements of the play influenced by any other work?
The structure wasn't inspired directly by any other works. It is just a tried and true structure. One character wants something specific and something stands in her way. She must figure out how to solve the problem and ends up a changed person at the end. In the Western part of the world, this is a pretty typical approach to drama. Using the structure usually creates a strong story.

Have you dealt with the same theme in other works that you have written?
Most of my plays have female protagonists, and many of them focus on female friendships. When I try to write a play with a male protagonist, the female characters usually turn out to be more interesting. Feminism and girl power are themes in most (okay, maybe all) of my plays. All of the plays that I have written for high school students focus on sports. I didn't do that on purpose, but now I realize that female characters who play sports are often strong and gutsy.

What writers have had the most profound effect on your style?
My first playwright love is Tennessee Williams. He was initially my inspiration, but as I've gotten older, the writer who has had the biggest effect on my style is Sarah Ruhl. I admire her female protagonists, poetic dialogue, and subtle magical realism. I am a total fangirl for so many contemporary women playwrights who push boundaries and have innovative styles. Young Jean Lee, Ruth Margraff, Suzan Lori-Parks, Lynn Nottage, Lydia R. Diamond, Quiara Alegría Hudes, and Janine Nabers are some of my favorites.

What do you hope to achieve with this work?
Most importantly, I want to write complex roles for teenagers to play. I don't like seeing teenagers playing people outside of their age range because high school is one of the most compelling times in our lives, and therefore, I want to tell those stories. When I write plays for young actors, I want to provide opportunities for students to tell realistic stories that don't involve stereotypes.

What were the biggest challenges involved in the writing of this play?
Honestly, for me, the biggest challenge involved in writing any play is finding the time to do it. I teach at a college full-time and teach and write at the Alliance Theatre. I am also co-artistic director of Found Stages Theatre. I love all of these parts of my life so much that I don't want to give up any of them. I also have a daughter who is in the sixth grade and never want work to take time away from her. Therefore, time management becomes so important. I am lucky that my husband is supportive of my writing and is willing to take over the parenting on Saturday afternoons so that I can go to the coffee shop and write.

What are the most common mistakes that occur in productions of your work?
I have to say that I have liked most of the productions of my plays. Some have been done by Equity actors, but others are done by students. When high school or middle school student actors, directors, and designers do my plays, I don't think that the actual production quality is important. Instead, I hope that students use my plays as a learning tool. Therefore, I don't mind "mistakes." They are a necessary teaching tool and cause growth.

What inspired you to become a playwright?
When I was a freshman in high school, I took a beginning theatre class.

They needed someone short to play the little sister in *Meet Me in St. Louis*. I've never been over five feet tall, which allowed me to get the part and move to the advanced theatre class. I fell in love and knew at fourteen that I wanted to tell stories through theatre but wasn't quite sure if I would do it through acting, tech, directing, or writing. When I was applying for colleges, I decided that writing was the path that best suited me. I then began the theatre/playwriting program at Marymount Manhattan College and have been writing ever since.

How did you research the subject?
Although none of them ended up directly inspiring my play, my eleven-year-old daughter and I watched a lot of promposal videos on YouTube. Because my play is about rejection, I also watched videos of promposal failures. While it's not formal research, being around high school students helps me with language and tone. I have taught playwriting camps at the Alliance Theatre and teach older teenagers at Georgia State University. The students at the Alliance have taught me so

much; for example, they don't like plays that talk down to them.

Are any characters modeled after real life or historical figures?

My lifelong best friend and I can give each other the courage to do just about anything. We even moved to New York together when we were eighteen. We have always encouraged each other to take risks, and because we've always known that the other one would be supportive whether we succeeded or failed, we have both been able to live our lives with a certain kind of courage. Our friendship inspired Carly and Mara. They have a kind of bravery together that they would not have on their own.

What is your writing process?

When I come up with an idea for a play, I usually don't start writing right away. I call it becoming pregnant with a play. I think about the play and come up with ideas for quite a while before I begin writing. Because of this, when I start the actual writing process, it goes fairly quickly. I start by writing a short draft of the play. It contains all of the plot points and is a complete play, but it lacks development and the characters are not fleshed out. I then go back and develop the play and the characters further. The draft then becomes much more detailed and the characters are more developed. After a more complete draft, I have an informal reading, then do rewrites based on what I hear. After that draft, I have a more formal reading/workshop and then do another rewrite. I then give the script to my trusted friend and dramaturg and receive feedback from him. He always finds new ways to think about the play that I would have never seen; I always rewrite based on his suggestions.

Shakespeare gave advice to the players in *Hamlet*; if you could give advice to your cast what would it be?
The reason I write plays, as opposed to any other medium, is because I like the collaboration involved in theatre. So collaborate! Add layers of meaning and individuality to the text. I only write the play. It is up to those working on the production to interpret the story through directing, design, and acting. You are students, so learning should be at the core of the experience. And don't forget to have fun.

About the Author

Neeley Gossett holds an MFA from The Playwright's Lab at Hollins University. Her works have received productions and readings at the Alliance Theatre, 7 Stages, Lark Play Development Center, Manhattan Repertory Theatre, Onstage Atlanta, The Coastal Empire New Play Festival, The Great Plains Theatre Conference, Mill Mountain Theater, Riverside Theatre, The Atlanta History Center, One Minute Play Festival Atlanta, The University of West Georgia, and other theatres. Her plays, *As U Like It* and *Carolina Dive*, are published by YouthPLAYS. Neeley has an M.A. in English from The University of North Carolina Wilmington and a B.A. in Theater from Marymount Manhattan College. She works as a Teaching Artist at the Alliance Theatre and an English Instructor at Georgia State University Perimeter College. She is a co-founder of Found Stages, through which her immersive play, *Beulah Creek* premiered and was nominated for The Suzi Bass Awards' Gene-Gabriel Moore Playwriting Award.

FORMING BONDS

A short comedy by
Ricky Young-Howze

CAST OF CHARACTERS

JENNIFER, 17, female, senior. A mousy girl. Honor student.
Lab Rat.

MASON, 17, male, senior. A cross-country runner. Prays for a
C+ average. Jock.

SETTING

A school library.

(In blackout we hear JENNIFER and MASON speaking.)

JENNIFER: You have four seconds to get these things off of me before I chew my own arm off!

MASON: I'm sorry... This trick always works on the internet.

JENNIFER: What in the world are you trying to do to me?

MASON: They were supposed to come off.

(The lights come up and we see Jennifer and Mason sitting at a library table. They are handcuffed together. Mason has a magic wand in his other hand. He puts a towel over their hands and waves the wand over it.)

Ego sum gelata liba!

(He pulls off the towel and the handcuffs are still there. He tries the trick one more time.)

Ego sum gelata liba!

(He pulls off the towel. No luck.)

JENNIFER: What's your endgame here? Because if you want to show up to your chemistry test with a black eye I can finish the magic trick for you.

(She takes the magic wand from him and starts to hit him with it.)

MASON: If you will stop hitting me I'll tell you.

JENNIFER: You have five seconds.

MASON: I was supposed to put the handcuffs on you then wave my magic wand...

JENNIFER: Skip ahead, I saw that part.

MASON: And it was supposed to transform into this.

(Mason pulls a corsage out of his pocket and holds it up for her to see.)

JENNIFER: Wait…is that a corsage?

MASON: Yes…and it was supposed to magically show up on your wrist. And I was supposed to get down on one knee…which is where I happen to be…and say, "Jennifer, will you go to prom with me?"

JENNIFER: You bought that?

MASON: Yes.

JENNIFER: You have to be kidding. Just for me?

MASON: All for you… Jennifer, will you go to prom with me?

JENNIFER: *(Sweetly:)* Awww…

(Beat. She shakes her head to regain her senses and then starts hitting him with the wand again.)

If you don't stop playing games with me, you won't even live till prom!!!

MASON: I can live with that.

(He looks around and suddenly grabs Jennifer in his arms.)

JENNIFER: Let go of me!

MASON: People are looking at us. If we get in trouble and my dad finds out that I stole his spare handcuffs, I'm dead.

JENNIFER: Is your dad a cop?

MASON: Yeah.

JENNIFER: Can I call him to report a potential murder?

MASON: He'll be happy to help you if we get caught.

JENNIFER: Mason, if we're seen like this, people will think we're together.

MASON: What's wrong with that?

JENNIFER: Do you really want to lose your cheerleader fan club? If they see us like this, I'll never hear the end of it.

MASON: I don't have a fan club.

JENNIFER: Please, you're like candy to them.

MASON: You never said if you're going to prom with me.

JENNIFER: Come on, stop fooling! We don't like the same things. You...Jock. Me...Not.

MASON: But we spent so much time together getting ready for the test...

JENNIFER: Yeah, tutor, I do that for a lot of people.

MASON: But...but chemistry.

JENNIFER: I help a lot of people with chemistry.

MASON: No, I was starting to think that maybe we had chemistry.

(Jennifer smirks and starts laughing.)

Wait, what?

JENNIFER: So you like want to go out with me?

MASON: Yeah, but—

JENNIFER: My idea of a romantic evening is looking through a microscope and curling up with the latest issue of *Popular Science*. Do you really want to make a hypothesis with me?

MASON: Well, not on the first date. I'm a gentleman.

JENNIFER: And you probably watch everything you eat... All natural, good carbs and everything?

MASON: Well yeah...

JENNIFER: I drink a river of orange soda every night. And frozen pizza. You really wanna eat pizza with me?

MASON: You fascinate me.

JENNIFER: Really? I doubt it, but thank you.

(She looks around and quickly hides behind Mason using him as a shield.)

Oh my god! A group of girls is looking at us.

MASON: Why would they be looking at us?

JENNIFER: Have you looked at you? You're everything they want. Go date them.

MASON: I don't want to date them. I want to date you.

(Mason walks himself over until they are out of sight. He spins around. Jennifer finds herself face to face with Mason. Mason leans in and tries to kiss her. She shoves her hand in his face.)

JENNIFER: Uh...no!

MASON: Sorry. I just...I can't even think when I'm around you. It's like, when I look at you, I feel like my heart is in one of those centrifuges in the lab. You got me spinning.

(Jennifer swirls her arm around until she is choking him with his own arm.)

JENNIFER: Look, I've heard about this happening with other tutors. What you have here is a textbook case of transference. You came here for the brain, and you're trying to trick yourself into thinking that you like everything else too. Now I know I'm fabulous, but I'm not what you like.

MASON: What are you trying to say?

JENNIFER: It's all in your head, you big dummy! There is just no way that you can be this smitten with me.

MASON: Why not?

JENNIFER: I'm not all bouncy and flirty and hot. I'm just Jen.

MASON: You can't really mean that.

JENNIFER: Just get the keys and cut me loose.

MASON: Don't you know you're cute?

JENNIFER: Stop it.

(Mason turns himself around out of the chokehold.)

MASON: You're really interesting.

JENNIFER: Don't—

MASON: Why don't you ever come out to the tailgates? Guys would be falling all over themselves.

JENNIFER: I don't do tailgates. I have class—

MASON: Who signs up for more science class?

(Jennifer pushes him off of her.)

JENNIFER: No—I have Combat Hapkido at the learning annex. And I'm training for my black belt test. So do you want to keep playing around or…?

MASON: We could have fun.

JENNIFER: I don't think that would be possible.

MASON: I think you could be lots of fun if you tried.

(Jennifer grabs him by the shoulders and starts to shake him.)

JENNIFER: Just get the keys and get me out of here!

MASON: Okay, they're in my backpack. On the key chain.

(Jennifer goes to his backpack and fumbles for the keys. She dumps everything on the floor.)

It's in the zipper pocket.

JENNIFER: There are a million zippers!

MASON: I just want to…be studied by you some more.

JENNIFER: Excuse me?

(He finds the key instantly and unlocks her. He looks into her eyes.)

MASON: You changed me.

JENNIFER: What?

MASON: You were like that guy Hindenburg.

JENNIFER: What are you talking about?

MASON: That guy that said that whatever you study you also change?

JENNIFER: You mean Heisenberg?

MASON: Yeah, him. When I first started tutoring with you, I thought I was one way. And then when you started looking at me I found out I was different. I'm...seeing things now, about myself, that I never saw before.

JENNIFER: We never covered Heisenberg. It's not even on the test. How do you know this?

(He picks up a book that fell on the floor.)

MASON: He was in this book that I saw you reading. I checked it out when you turned it back in.

JENNIFER: You read advanced theory in Physics?

MASON: I'm having new thoughts now. I mean, I run...all you have to do is run. Now when I run, I'm looking at the steam coming up off the pavement and I'm seeing water molecules and evaporation. I have a brain now.

JENNIFER: You always had a brain, you idiot.

MASON: Can you help me find it? I think I lost it a long time ago.

JENNIFER: Just because you don't see the truth in yourself doesn't mean that others can't see it in you.

(Mason looks at her, knowingly.)

Oh, I'm such an idiot. You were saying that you...and me...

MASON: I knew you would get it if you really thought about it.

(Mason picks up the corsage and puts it on her wrist.)

Come to the prom with me?

JENNIFER: I... I don't know what to say. Are you sure? I'm sure you could have more fun without me.

MASON: There's something so much better than fun.

JENNIFER: What?

MASON: Chemistry.

(He moves to kiss her again. She stops him.)

JENNIFER: You really didn't just say that.

(Pause. She leans and kisses him lightly on the lips.)

(Lights out.)

(End of play.)

The Author Speaks

What inspired you to write this play?
I was always the awkward kid in school and a bit of an old soul. When I started writing this play I knew two things: That I didn't really know what "promposing" was, and that if this had been popular when I was a kid I certainly would have messed it up. So after using my two teen cousins for research, I started from the idea of a promposal gone wrong. What would have to happen then?

Was the structure or other elements of the play influenced by any other work?
The idea of two people being handcuffed together has been comedy gold for over a century. I've seen it done in black and white movies, cartoons from my childhood, and even today's sitcoms. Most handcuff scenes deal with physical comedy. I wanted to try a scene that balanced physical comedy, wit, and feeling. I wanted the give and take of dialogue to be just as important as the physical action.

Have you dealt with the same theme in other works that you have written?
I often like to deal with feelings of love and friendship "after the fact." Too many plays try to keep up tension with a "will they or won't they?" I start with people saying "we are, now what?" or "oh no I have feelings but that's bad." I also like dealing with clumsy romances where no one says the right thing and things don't get resolved exactly like you planned. Call it "dorky love" if you will.

What writers have had the most profound effect on your style?
Neil Simon is a writer that I always go back to. He is the master of how comedy works on stage and how "comedy" and "seriousness" aren't mortal enemies. I was also nurtured as a

young playwright by Cherie Bennett and Jeff Gottesfeld. They taught me that you can bring modern issues and language onstage and not only do what teens want to be in them, but what audiences want to see them.

What do you hope to achieve with this work?
I hope that teens know that it's okay to be a little bit dorky. Even if nothing goes right, speaking from the heart is always a good idea.

What were the biggest challenges involved in the writing of this play?
The biggest challenge was tapping into Jennifer's character. I wrote a couple drafts that involved Jennifer being more withdrawn and "mousy" or exploring her character as a science nerd. Jennifer couldn't be one-note because modern teens aren't one-note "nerdy" or "jock." In later drafts I feel I dialed in to a more aggressive Jennifer who loves science and Combat Hapkido but still doesn't feel like she's the right fit for a "jock" like Mason.

What are the most common mistakes that occur in productions of your work?
The most common mistake is wanting to rush through the dialogue. Second to that is not tackling the scene with enough energy. I write characters who take everything at a hundred percent, and I feel that I can tell when an actor is only playing at eighty percent.

What inspired you to become a playwright?
I was inspired mostly by the husband of my high school theatre teacher. He has written twenty of the best plays that will never see publishing or the recognition that they deserve. I also have him and my theatre teacher to thank for taking my first play that I sent them and giving it a production. From a very early age, I learned the joy of writing dialogue for two

actors on stage and letting the story unfold between them. It was his work that taught me that joy.

How did you research the subject?

I have two teen cousins that field a lot of questions for me. Usually they end up sounding like "is this still cool?" or "is this still a thing anymore?" I normally keep myself surrounded by friends, teachers, and family members that remind me that I'm technically old.

What is your writing process?

I start by journaling most days. While I'm writing or reading through other journals, I'll have a story idea come to me. This could be a cool image or theme, a line that gets stuck in my head, or a short scene that starts playing in my head and won't come out. Then I start making notes and outlines until I can picture the whole play in my head or at least know how it will end. Then those notes lay around in my bag or on my desk until I sit down and write the draft over the course of a day or week.

By this time the play is nowhere near done. I normally take the draft into a workshop process with people I trust and rewrite about three or four times until it's perfect. The process this play went through was unique because I had an idea locked down and went into the draft stage really quickly. I had a trusted group of people helping me through the draft process and I was able to get through that quickly too.

Shakespeare gave advice to the players in *Hamlet*; if you could give advice to your cast what would it be?

Take your time with the dialogue and don't rush. Tackle the characters with 100% energy and make every choice with full energy too.

Why do you write?

I always felt like I was an awkward kid. When I was creating a story, I could build a world where I always said or did the right thing. I found that I communicated my feelings better to people when I wrote a poem or an essay. Plays gave me the best of both worlds. I can create worlds onstage where my fellow "awkward" people can get their moment, and I can share a part of me that people don't see otherwise. For me, this form of expression is one of the most vital ways I have to communicate with other people.

About the Author

Ricky Young-Howze is a playwright and theatre writer from New Jersey. He is a transplant from Tennessee, where he graduated from Austin Peay State University with a B. S. in Theatre Performance and a minor in design. There he was awarded the honor of "Most Outstanding Exiting Senior of Theatre and Dance." He holds an MFA from the Playwright's Lab at from Hollins University.

THE WATER TOWER

A short dramedy by
Will Coleman

CAST OF CHARACTERS

DAMON, male, 18, a high school senior.

RICHARD, male, 17, a junior. Damon's best friend.

(The top of the water tower. DAMON and RICHARD aren't really supposed to be there.)

(They are, though.)

(Richard appears, carrying some binoculars, followed by Damon, who, exhausted from climbing the ladder to the top, lies face down, but only for a second.)

DAMON: Oh, it's hot! This was a bad idea, bad idea! It's a big metal sheet baking in the sun all day!

(Damon jumps up, trying to soothe his burned face.)

RICHARD: Oh, c'mon, it's worth it though.

DAMON: Climbing the water tower?

RICHARD: I think so.

DAMON: I guess we'll find out, won't we?

RICHARD: I'm confident.

DAMON: You sure you just haven't watched too many YouTube videos?

RICHARD: I may have.

DAMON: Couldn't you just lip sync to Bruno Mars [any current, terrible singer will do fine here] like a normal person?

RICHARD: Hold your tongue.

DAMON: It would've been a lot easier.

RICHARD: Everybody does that. I wanted to do something different.

DAMON: Of course you do. I just hope it works.

RICHARD: No, it's gonna be great. The surprise is the best part.

DAMON: What time does she get here?

RICHARD: Not for another hour or so.

DAMON: What? Then what are we doing here?

RICHARD: I had to test it out.

DAMON: Oh, so I'm your guinea pig?

RICHARD: Every day.

DAMON: Thanks.

RICHARD: You're sure you don't want to ask anyone?

DAMON: If I wanted to ask anyone to prom, I would just do it, I wouldn't go through all the...pomp.

RICHARD: I don't know what that word means.

DAMON: I know.

RICHARD: But there wasn't anyone you wanted to ask?

DAMON: Not really.

RICHARD: Not even Brad Minor?

DAMON: Don't get me started on Brad Minor.

RICHARD: I thought you liked him.

DAMON: He's just a little too high school.

RICHARD: Oh, so you're over all that now?

DAMON: There's a lot more important things to worry about.

RICHARD: Okay, okay. It's just...it's your senior prom. This is your last chance.

DAMON: Trust me, I'm just looking forward to college at this point.

RICHARD: Serious, intellectual guys?

DAMON: Sure. And questioning football players, away from their conservative hometowns for the first time...

RICHARD: Okay, I get it.

DAMON: So prom's not that big a deal for me.

RICHARD: Not what you said last year—

DAMON: Plus, I'm leaving in August. It's not like I'm gonna start a relationship now...

RICHARD: ...yeah.

DAMON: Oh, man. Sorry, Richard.

RICHARD: No, it's cool.

DAMON: I mean, Charlotte is pretty cool, and she's just gonna be what, three hours away? That's not that bad.

RICHARD: She can come home on weekends.

DAMON: Sure.

RICHARD: Could be worse.

DAMON: I'm sorry.

RICHARD: No, it's cool. Not like she's gonna be all the way in New York.

DAMON: Yeah.

RICHARD: Like some other people.

DAMON: I know.

RICHARD: I guess I'll have to make some friends my own age.

DAMON: Or just suffer through it until you move to New York next year.

RICHARD: And I have all year to sell my parents on that idea.

DAMON: I didn't mean to bring it up.

RICHARD: It's alright. Hey, let's check the signs out.

(Richard gives Damon the binoculars.)

DAMON: This is elaborate.

(Richard texts someone.)

RICHARD: Check the roof of the band building.

(Damon scans with the binoculars.)

DAMON: Hey! It's Stuart. He's holding a sign that says, "ready."

RICHARD: Awesome. That means everybody's in position. I hope they got the order right.

DAMON: Well, there's plenty of time to try over and over again before she gets here. In the blistering, oppressive heat.

RICHARD: Right.

(Richard sends another text message.)

DAMON: Where to?

RICHARD: Keep it there. It should flip over right...now.

DAMON: It says, "Hey."

RICHARD: Okay, so now over to the roof of the movie theater.

DAMON: "I know you're leaving next year..."

RICHARD: The used bookstore.

DAMON: "...and I wanted you to know, before you go..."

RICHARD: El Matador.

DAMON: "...how much you mean to me."

RICHARD: Ponder Auto.

DAMON: "I love you." Damn, dude.

RICHARD: Band building again.

DAMON: "And it's going to be difficult without you here."

RICHARD: Movie theater.

DAMON: "So I think that we should have one last hurrah." Hurrah? Dude. Lame.

RICHARD: Bookstore.

DAMON: "Because I know you're going to miss high school more than you let on."

RICHARD: El Matador.

DAMON: "A lot of memories in those halls."

RICHARD: Ponder Auto.

DAMON: "So let's make one more. One last one."

RICHARD: Band building.

DAMON: "You're my best friend."

(Damon just now starts to get it.)

RICHARD: Theater.

DAMON: "There's no one else I'd rather go with."

RICHARD: Bookstore.

DAMON: "So, please go to prom with me."

RICHARD: El Matador.

DAMON: "In case you're extra dense today,"

RICHARD: Ponder Auto.

DAMON: "I'm talking to you, Damon."

(He puts the binoculars down.)

(Richard is holding out a boutonniere.)

RICHARD: So?

DAMON: Oh, shut up.

(Damon is deeply touched, but would never let Richard know that.)

RICHARD: I'm serious.

DAMON: You're such an idiot.

RICHARD: Yeah.

DAMON: What about Charlotte?

RICHARD: Charlotte's totally cool with it. She's gonna go with Jessica. It'll be a whole thing, together, but... This isn't about Charlotte. This is about me and you. And I know you want to go to prom, you can't pass up an opportunity to Whip and/or Nae Nae. [Any reference to a lame dance done at proms and weddings will work here.]

DAMON: True. But I'm not some sad, gay charity case, Richard.

RICHARD: I know. It's not about that. It's about me wanting to go to prom with my best friend. That's all.

DAMON: Is that a boutonniere?

RICHARD: It is.

DAMON: That is going to be seriously dead. Prom is in three weeks.

RICHARD: It was more of a symbol.

DAMON: You're more of a symbol.

RICHARD: Yeah.

(Damon takes the boutonniere, and, not knowing what to do, puts it in his pocket.)

DAMON: Alright.

RICHARD: That a yes?

DAMON: I mean, since you're clearly so desperate.

RICHARD: Cool.

DAMON: Thanks.

(Richard hugs him.)

Too much, too much!

RICHARD: Just let me love you!

(Damon reluctantly hugs him back.)

DAMON: Can we get off this death trap now?

RICHARD: Deal.

DAMON: That was super gay, by the way.

RICHARD: I know.

DAMON: Like, I've never done anything that gay.

RICHARD: I know.

DAMON: And I, like, get it on with dudes.

RICHARD: Okay.

(They walk offstage.)

(End of play.)

The Author Speaks

What inspired you to write this play?
An idea shared by another playwright, on a topic I had only heard about in passing: a promposal. After a quick search on YouTube, I found out it was wildly popular, and something that I would have been very into in high school, with my penchant for the theatrical, of course. So, in a first for me, the play is set in the town where I went to high school, with the landmarks one should be able to see from a specific water tower I had in mind. That part was fun to write, and I hope someone may recognize it one day.

Have you dealt with the same theme in other works that you have written?
I think all of my plays are a similar style, in that I'm a strong believer in comedy and emotion mixed together, and sweetness undercut by irony. Richard is very sincere, and Damon has a layer of irony over an emotional core. The idea of people resisting a real, emotional moment is something that I see in real life constantly, and I try to recreate that in my plays.

What writers have had the most profound effect on your style?
I'm not really sure if this is apparent in this particular work, but Caryl Churchill is my favorite playwright, and I love her sense of the theatrical. All of her plays have something in them that can only be done, or at least work best, on stage, as opposed to any other medium. Her plays tend to be very dark, but with a lot of humor and whimsical elements in them, and that's something that I try to keep in my own work.

What do you hope to achieve with this work?
A conversation about friendship and what memories you make in high school, I think. Is prom a tired tradition that has

no place in our culture or our memories? Or is it just a night for you to spend with the people that you care about, some of whom you may not see again?

What were the biggest challenges involved in the writing of this play?
As always, trying to make the characters believable and relatable, despite the heightened circumstances of what they're doing, because if they don't seem like real people, then I haven't done my job.

What inspired you to become a playwright?
Reading and seeing plays. I've always been writing, and I still write prose, but my real discovery of theatre in high school inspired me to try writing plays as well. I've never really stopped since then.

How did you research the subject?
I watched some videos of promposals on YouTube to get a baseline for what was common, and most of them consisted of flash mobs or lip-syncing to pop songs, some more elaborate than others. I tried to think of something I would have done when I was in high school, and that's where the idea came from.

Are any characters modeled after real life or historical figures?
Not specifically, but the central relationship comes from my own high school experience, as my best friend came out of the closet in ninth grade. In school it wasn't a big deal, he wasn't bullied or anything (maybe because he could have kicked their butts), but his parents had a real problem with it. In tenth grade they sent him six hours away to a very conservative boarding school, and although I did see him again, we were never really as close. So when I started thinking about how I

would have done a promposal in high school, that relationship jumped to mind.

What is your writing process?
I try to write early in the morning, if I can, and in a public place. If I'm in a coffee shop, I have fewer distractions and more of an impetus to actually write. I'll give myself a goal for the day, like a scene I want to finish, and tell myself I can't go home until I've completed my goal. I also listen to music when I write, and try to select something with a mood similar to what I'm writing, usually instrumental, but not always.

Shakespeare gave advice to the players in *Hamlet*; if you could give advice to your cast what would it be?
For the actor playing Damon, remember that he has a lot of conflicting emotions right now. Richard is his best friend, and he's going to miss him, but he also can't wait to get out of this small town and move to New York. He's always thought prom was a waste of time, but the idea of a big party with all of his friends, "one last hurrah," as lame as it sounds, is attractive, although he doesn't want to admit it.

For the actor playing Richard, try to remember that the two closest people to him are both going to be gone for his senior year: his best friend and his girlfriend. And they're going to be far away. He has already made the decision that he wants to make prom about his friendship with Damon, and he's a direct, emotional person, unlike Damon, but he knows him well enough to know that Damon cares about these things, too. Try to draw that out.

About the Author

Will Coleman is the artistic director of The Wheelhouse Theatre in Chicago. His play *Helvetica* won the Getchell New Play Award from SETC, and was chosen for Applause's *Best*

Festival Plays of 2015 anthology. Other plays include **Krugozor!, The Brooklyn Bridge (and other marvels), A Crack in a Wall,** and the musicals **Zombie Boyfriend!** and **Squid Hunt!**. He is currently an MFA candidate at the Playwright's Lab at Hollins University.

ANTE UP

A short comedy by
Laura King

CAST OF CHARACTERS

JORY, a female high school senior. A hipster, although she's tiring of it.

GINO, a male high school senior. A hipster, although he'd never admit it.

SETTING

A high school gymnasium.

(Lights up on a high school gymnasium. JORY is hanging fuzzy dice. GINO is shuffling a deck of cards.)

GINO: Worst. Detention. Ever.

JORY: It's not so bad.

GINO: Prom prep? Who gives someone prom prep for detention?

JORY: Let the punishment fit the crime.

GINO: All we did was deface some prom posters.

JORY: What's all this *we* stuff?

GINO: Okay, me. You lost your nerve.

JORY: I did not. I just didn't see the point.

GINO: Why are you even here? *I* got detention.

JORY: I'm here for moral support. I'm your best friend, remember?

GINO: Well, thanks, buddy, but since you don't have to be here and I don't want to be here, I say we split.

JORY: We have to finish decorating. Put those cards away and come help me.

GINO: Deal me out.

(Gino starts to leave but Jory stops him.)

JORY: You can't leave. You'll get in trouble.

GINO: I'll take my chances.

JORY: Come on, Gino. We're almost done. Soon this place will look just like a casino.

GINO: The Viva Las Vegas Prom. Whose brilliant idea was that? Let's transform the gym into Vegas so the seniors can look forward to all the gambling, drinking, and strip clubs in their future.

JORY: Stop being so cynical. It's better than the other ideas: Masquerade —

GINO: I could disguise myself as somebody who actually gives a crap.

JORY: Or Enchantment Under the Sea.

GINO: Drown me.

JORY: It could be fun.

GINO: What? Prom?

JORY: A last chance to hang with everybody.

GINO: You mean graze with everybody.

JORY: Here we go.

GINO: Look, Jory, if you want to be just another sheep herded into this pen and forced to conform to the ways of the other livestock, go for it, but count me out.

JORY: Fine! Then you can count me out of your detention.

(Jory slams down the fuzzy dice.)

GINO: What are you so mad about?

JORY: *(Yelling:)* I'm not mad!

GINO: Then why are you yelling?

JORY: Because I came here to tell you something, but you're impossible to talk to.

GINO: But you put up with me anyway.

JORY: Don't ask me why.

GINO: Friends for life. That's what you promised.

JORY: I was in second grade.

(Gino lifts his pinky and crosses to Jory. She begrudgingly locks pinkies with Gino.)

JORY: Cross my heart and hear me cry, we'll be friends until we die.

GINO: Cross my heart and hear me cry, we'll be friends until we die.

GINO: Come on. Let's cash out.

JORY: You've got another ten minutes.

GINO: I refuse to compromise my beliefs one more second.

JORY: Which belief of your oh-so-many beliefs are you referring to?

GINO: The myth of prom.

JORY: One of your top ten.

GINO: Go to prom, you'll fit in. Go to prom, you'll be successful. Go to prom, you'll be happy for the rest of your life.

JORY: Is that all it takes?

GINO: It's a load of bull.

JORY: I know, but—

GINO: But what? You know I'm right.

JORY: Aren't you always?

GINO: What's wrong with you today?

JORY: Nothing.

GINO: *(Teasing Jory:)* Are you having *prom*blems?

JORY: *(Smiling:)* Shut up.

GINO: Is all the *prom*a getting to you?

JORY: *(Laughing:)* Knock it off.

GINO: Are you sad because you haven't had a *prom*posal?

JORY: *(Stops laughing:)* I've got to go.

GINO: Wait. I thought we had to finish decorating.

JORY: Do it yourself.

GINO: But you came to help.

JORY: That's not why I came.

GINO: Then why? Come on, Jory. What's going on?

JORY: You'll just laugh.

GINO: *(Holding up his pinky:)* I won't. Pinky swear.

JORY: All right. I'm going.

GINO: Where?

JORY: To prom, you idiot.

GINO: Very funny. *(Pause.)* Jory? *(Pause.)* No way. You're going to prom?

JORY: Yes. I don't know. Maybe.

GINO: With who?

JORY: Marcus asked me.

GINO: Moron Marcus?

JORY: Don't call him that.

GINO: If he was any stupider, he'd have to be watered twice a week.

JORY: At least he does more than talk.

GINO: That's because he has nothing to say.

JORY: He's nice. I've been tutoring him in English. He listens to me.

GINO: He's white-bread, bourgeois, and middle-class.

JORY: We're white-bread, bourgeois, and middle-class.

GINO: Speak for yourself.

JORY: I'm speaking for you, Eugene Melman.

GINO: Don't call me that.

JORY: Why not? It's your given white-bread, bourgeois, middle-class name.

GINO: Fine, Marjorie Anne Taylor.

JORY: Nobody calls me that but my mother.

GINO: What about Moron Marcus? What does he call you? What did he say to get you to go to prom with him? Did he just grunt twice and point to the poster?

JORY: He asked. That's all. He just asked.

GINO: That's all it took?

JORY: Yes.

GINO: Then he must have better luck than me.

JORY: What are you talking about?

GINO: I can't believe you don't remember.

JORY: Remember what?

GINO: Ninth grade. Freshman mixer. Ring a bell?

JORY: No.

GINO: I asked you to go with me!

JORY: You did?

GINO: We were sitting right here in the gym on the bleachers. You were pretending you had sprained your ankle, and I was pretending to have the flu so we could skip PE.

JORY: Because the public school system doesn't have the right to make us physically active.

GINO: Exactly. Our bodies, our decisions. If we want to be fat, gluttonous slugs, that's our right.

JORY: Anyway...

GINO: Anyway, I asked you if you wanted to go.

JORY: What did I say?

GINO: You don't remember dancing with me, do you?

JORY: No.

GINO: Then obviously you said no. I swore I'd never ask you to anything ever again.

JORY: Is that why— Wait a minute. I remember. You didn't *ask* me ask me.

GINO: I did too.

JORY: You did not. You said, "You don't want to go to that stupid dance, do you?"

GINO: And you said no.

JORY: What was I supposed to say?

GINO: Yes!

JORY: So you could make fun of me for wanting to go?

GINO: I wouldn't do that.

JORY: You're making fun of me now.

GINO: I'm not... Okay, I am. I just don't get it.

JORY: I don't either really.

GINO: Why do you even want to go?

JORY: Why shouldn't I want to go? Because you don't think I should? I'm allowed to think for myself, you know. Believe it or not, I'm not a sheep.

GINO: I know.

JORY: I've been following you around since elementary school. Listening to you go on and on about what you believe, but I'm allowed to believe some stuff, too.

GINO: I know.

JORY: And it doesn't have to be the same stuff you believe.

GINO: I know. I'm sorry.

JORY: We're seniors. This is the end. I don't want to have any regrets. When I look back at high school, I don't want it to be only memories of sitting on the bleachers watching everybody else play. Is that what you want?

GINO: I don't know anymore.

(Jory and Gino are quiet for a bit. Jory looks at her watch.)

JORY: Detention is over.

GINO: I guess we can officially go.

(Jory picks up the fuzzy dice. Gino puts the cards back in their box.)

JORY: No more compromising your beliefs.

GINO: Yeah.

JORY: I'll see you, Gino.

GINO: See ya, Jory.

JORY: Gino.

GINO: What?

JORY: I didn't tell Marcus for sure I'd go.

GINO: You didn't?

JORY: I mean if somebody else asked me, he wouldn't have a problem finding another date.

GINO: That's for sure. His kind is in high demand.

JORY: Don't start.

GINO: If there's one thing the people in this school like it's the pedestrian.

JORY: Oh, man.

GINO: Let's all wallow in it. Let's cover ourselves in the mud of mediocrity and conform to the ideals of the mundane minions that roam these halls.

JORY: Gino.

GINO: Let's hang floating dice from the ceiling, pass out decks of cards as party favors, and dance around a fake slot machine with a moron who can't even spell the word prom.

JORY: Gino!

GINO: What?

JORY: Roll the dice.

(Jory tosses Gino the pair of fuzzy dice.)

GINO: What if I crap out again?

JORY: You won't.

GINO: *(Gathering his courage:)* Jory…

JORY: Yes?

GINO: Deal me in?

(Gino tosses Jory the deck of cards.)

JORY: I thought you'd never ask.

(Jory runs to Gino and throws her arms around him. They hug. Gino fist pumps.)

GINO: Jackpot!

(End of play.)

The Author Speaks

What inspired you to write this play?
I was taking a class at Hollins University on writing plays for young audiences. The class had just completed writing ten-minute plays about parental expectations, which was a particularly heavy subject. We all wanted to do something lighter, so we came up with the idea of writing plays about promposals. I decided to write about high schoolers who pretended not to care about prom but deep down kind of did because that's the kind of high schooler I was.

Was the structure or other elements of the play influenced by any other work?
Ten-minute plays usually have the same structure, which is to start the action of the play immediately, complicate the action, and then resolve it. In ten-minute plays, every word counts, which is why I enjoy reading and writing them. I learned a lot about writing ten-minute plays from reading Gary Garrison's book *A More Perfect 10*. I also enjoy reading collections of ten-minute plays, such as **Girls on the Brink** published by YouthPLAYS. I have written a collection of my own called **Youth on the Roof**, published by YouthPLAYS.

Have you dealt with the same theme in other works that you have written?
I often write about teenage characters who are struggling with changes to their beliefs. In **Ante Up,** Jory and Gino have been pretending to not care for so long that their relationship is thrown off balance when Jory suddenly begins to care. Both Gino and Jory have to decide if they want to hold on to the old patterns in their relationship or start new patterns. My collection **Youth on the Roof** tells similar stories. It is about high schoolers who are confronting their futures and asking themselves what kind of adults they want to be.

What do you hope to achieve with this work?

I hope to convey to teenage audiences that sometimes pretending not to care can keep you from finding real connections with people. It takes courage to try new things, but the rewards can be so great. In a small way, this play encourages teenagers to take risks. For Jory, it's admitting that she wants to go to prom. For Gino, it's admitting that he wants to ask Jory to prom.

What were the biggest challenges involved in the writing of this play?

It's always challenging for an older person to write for younger people. There is a huge sense of responsibility to get those characters right! Not only is it important to use the language of young people (without condescending to them), it is also important to write about subjects that resonate with them. I think the secret is to find those issues that are universal. I think we all know what it feels like to be afraid to tell someone our true feelings.

What inspired you to become a playwright?

I came to playwriting later than most writers, but I was always a "theatre kid." From the moment I was cast as the Cowardly Lion in *The Wizard of Oz* in the sixth grade, I was hooked! I have acted, directed, and taught for many years. About five years ago, I took a playwriting class just for fun. I loved it and continued to write. I decided to get my MFA in playwriting, and the work I have done at Hollins University has been some of the most rewarding of my life.

How did you research the subject?

My daughter was in high school when I wrote this play, and I talked to her a lot about proms and promposals. I was fascinated by how big a deal this was now (not like when I was in high school). I also spoke with a high school teacher who had a lot of experience helping his students with their promposals. I also did some research on the Internet about prom themes and promposal ideas. It's a whole industry unto itself!

What is your writing process?
I try to write my first draft without censoring myself. I write whatever pops into my mind, even if it's crazy! I like to see where my mind takes me. After I have completed the first draft, I think for a long time about what the play is really about — what do I want to say with this play? Then I complete a second draft with that question in mind. After that, I need to hear the play out loud, so I try to have a formal reading or at least have some friends or students read it out. Then I revise again. I often ask myself, "Are plays ever really finished?" I think the answer is no.

Shakespeare gave advice to the players in *Hamlet*; if you could give advice to your cast what would it be?
I always give the same advice: Have fun! If the actors are having fun, the audience usually will too. Forgotten lines, missing props, ripped costumes — almost everything can be forgiven if the actors are having a good time. Other than enjoying yourselves, my advice is to turn to the script when you are in doubt about something. Answers can always be found in the words of the play. Be true to them.

About the Author

Laura King is a member of the Playwright's Lab at Hollins University. She has had ten-minute plays produced across the country, including her youth plays *The Disappointments, The Dodo Pact, The Crackling Rainbow Comet, How Penny Got Her Pep Back, The Piggy Pit*, and *Tag*. She is the author of the full-length plays *Independence Day at Happy Meadows, The Harmony Baptist Church Ladies Auxiliary Christmas Jubilee, Fallout*, and *Blood Will Out*.

HASHTAG ADORABLE

A short comedy by
Samantha Macher

CAST OF CHARACTERS

ELIZABETH, female, 18, choir member.

OLLIE, male, 18, choir member.

ALEX, female, 18, scrapbook aficionado.

CHOIR MEMBERS, various ages and genders.

(A group of high schoolers in choir robes are walking out of their latest rehearsal. They're a nerdy group, but they're sweet, and enthusiastic. There are about six of them total. Among them are ELIZABETH, a senior and obviously the leader, and OLLIE, a cool, confident sixteen-year-old.)

ELIZABETH: You guys! That was great. I think we nailed it that time.

CHOIR 1: You think so?

ELIZABETH: Definitely. We were almost on pitch in that last song!

CHOIR 2: Almost! And Ollie's solo —

ELIZABETH: Was freakin' sweet. I had no idea you could sing like that.

OLLIE: Me neither. I guess that's what adrenaline will do.

ELIZABETH: I don't care how you did it, I'm just glad you did.

CHOIR 1: Are we still doing the "thing" tonight?

CHOIR 2: Shh!! It's supposed to be a secret.

CHOIR 1: Not to them.

CHOIR 2: Oh yeah —

ELIZABETH: Yes. We're still on, but not for a little bit. Do you guys mind giving me and Ollie just a second?

CHOIR 1: Yeah, we'll meet up with you later.

ELIZABETH: Thanks guys!

(The rest of the choir exits. OLLIE and Elizabeth are left alone.)

So... Do you think it's going to be good, or —

OLLIE: I think they're ready for tonight.

ELIZABETH: I know we've been practicing, but I'm still nervous. What if —

OLLIE: It'll be fine, I promise. You just have to trust us, Elizabeth.

ELIZABETH: I know, I know. And I do. I totally do, but I feel like this is my one shot and I don't want to blow it. You know what's at stake.

OLLIE: *(Coyly:)* I do.

ELIZABETH: Hold up. You do? How —

OLLIE: I asked Melinda last week.

ELIZABETH: NO!

(She punches him in the arm.)

OLLIE: Ow!

ELIZABETH: Ooh. Sorry. Wait. No I'm not. Tell me everything. How'd it go? What did you do? What did she say?

OLLIE: It went fine. I walked her to the parking lot and gave her a mixtape with a bunch of songs that reminded me of her —

ELIZABETH: A mixtape?

OLLIE: Her grandma's car only has a tape deck.

ELIZABETH: Whoa. Old school.

OLLIE: So I gave her the thing and we got in her car, and we sat in the front seat, and told her to play the first song — our song. While it played, I asked her to go to the prom with me.

(A huge smile crosses his face, while simultaneously, a scowl crosses Elizabeth's.)

ELIZABETH: Oh crap, Ollie!

OLLIE: What?!

ELIZABETH: That's SO SMOOTH! It's simple, and romantic —

OLLIE: It's definitely romantic.

ELIZABETH: Which means I'm completely overthinking the whole thing! This is all too much. It's WAY too much! Alex isn't going to be expecting this —

OLLIE: She'll be fine.

ELIZABETH: No! You had it all right. Keep it calm, keep it quiet.

OLLIE: Not everyone's love has to be quiet.

ELIZABETH: What are you, some kind of poet?

OLLIE: *(Beat.)* Yeah.

ELIZABETH: I never even thought I could ever be with someone like Alex. And today is the day I'm deciding to be with her, for real. In public.

OLLIE: Yeah. Really public. Like, really soon.

ELIZABETH: My parents are gonna kill me. I never even told them I was— I'm screwed. I'm dead. So dead. But she's worth it. Right?

OLLIE: You're asking me?

ELIZABETH: You're my best friend.

OLLIE: You know I can't answer that —

ELIZABETH: Try!

OLLIE: FINE! Jeez. I can't tell you if I think she's worth it. But I think *you're* worth it. I always thought you should be who you are.

ELIZABETH: But what if —

OLLIE: Any question that starts with "what if" is stupid.

(ALEX, an outgoing, sporty girl, enters.)

Hi.

(Elizabeth takes a moment to take in how beautiful Alex looks right then in that moment. The world stops for just a second.)

ALEX: Hi.

ELIZABETH: Ollie, can you give us a sec?

OLLIE: Sure. Are we still on for the...

ELIZABETH: Yeah, yeah. Just. Wait for me, will ya?

OLLIE: You got it.

ALEX: Wait for you for what?

ELIZABETH: Nothing.

ALEX: No, what?

(Elizabeth takes Alex's hands in hers. Ollie exits.)

What are you guys planning?

ELIZABETH: Who says we're planning anything?

ALEX: Oh, right. Like you and Ollie aren't ALWAYS scheming something. What is it this time? A flash mob in chemistry class?

ELIZABETH: You plan ONE flash mob and suddenly you're the queen of flash mobs.

ALEX: Pulling the fire alarm during your French test?

ELIZABETH: Hey, I'm good at French. I don't need to pull the fire alarm.

ALEX: Well, whatever it is, I'm sure it'll be a shock to everyone.

ELIZABETH: Is that a good thing?

ALEX: *(Laughing:)* Well, you know I like surprises. Which is why I have one for you.

(Alex puts her backpack on the ground and pulls out a book.)

ELIZABETH: What's this?

ALEX: Take a look.

(Alex hands her a photo album. Elizabeth leafs through it.)

ELIZABETH: It's us.

ALEX: Yeah. I've really been enjoying the last few months together, and I thought, you know, maybe I'd throw some of those dumb selfies in a scrapbook.

ELIZABETH: Hashtag adorable.

ALEX: Hashtag crafting.

ELIZABETH: Hashtag... I'm out of hashtags.

(Elizabeth flips to the first page.)

Ooh! There's the one from the night we went to the party at Frida's house.

ALEX: Was that Halloween?

ELIZABETH: Nah. Just my femme fatale phase.

ALEX: That was a good phase— Look! There's the one from the ice skating rink from our first official-unofficial-secret date.

ELIZABETH: Oh man, I had forgotten how cold it was that day.

ALEX: And how bad you are at skating! You basically clung on to me the whole time.

ELIZABETH: Like you minded.

ALEX: Touché.

ELIZABETH: Oh! And there's one from the band and choir spring break competition trip!

ELIZABETH: We're so gross! Look at those bow ties.

ALEX: I'm more offended by the cummerbund, personally.

(Elizabeth flips through the pages.)

Look, there's a bunch more in here, and there's so many really good memories we could spend all day looking at, but I know your folks are coming soon to pick you up, and I wanted to make sure you saw this before you go.

(Alex turns to the last page.)

ELIZABETH: It's empty.

ALEX: I know. I'm hoping that's where we can put our prom picture.

ELIZABETH: What?

ALEX: Look, I know that we're still kind of keeping this whole thing on the down low, but I'm hoping that if I put on a dress and do the whole "hair and makeup" thing, your parents won't have too many questions if we go together as *(In air quotes:)* "friends."

(Elizabeth looks around nervously.)

ELIZABETH: Are you asking me to prom?

ALEX: I am.
I'm asking.
Will you go with me, Elizabeth?

ELIZABETH: Oh man.

ALEX: What? Is something wrong?

ELIZABETH: Not exactly.

ALEX: Because if you want, we can forget the whole thing —

ELIZABETH: No, that's not it.

ALEX: Well, then what is it?

ELIZABETH: It's just—

ALEX: If you don't want to go with me fine, but—

ELIZABETH: Wait—

ALEX: What?

ELIZABETH: I have to ask you a question.

(Elizabeth looks around expectantly.)

ALEX: What is it?

ELIZABETH: *(Loudly:)* I SAID "I HAVE TO ASK YOU A QUESTION."

ALEX: I'm standing right here.

ELIZABETH: I SAID—

(A rustle offstage as the choir comes back on in their usual disorganized fashion, led by Ollie.)

OLLIE: We heard you the second time. Jeez.

ALEX: What is this?

ELIZABETH: Alex, the time we've been together has been so special to me. I can't imagine high school, or even this part of my life without you. And today, even though you totally stole my thunder with that freaking amazing scrapbook, I want to ask you in front of everyone if you'll go to prom with me. With the real me who doesn't want to live one more second of my life being someone I'm not.

ALEX: Really? Elizabeth, this is so. It's so.

ELIZABETH: Surprising?

ALEX: That's one word for it.

(The choir strikes up. They're a little off pitch, but again, sweet and enthusiastic.)

WHOLE CHOIR: *(To the tune of "Oh! Susanna!":)* OH MY ALEX
PLEASE GO TO PROM WITH ME
I WILL BUY YOU A CORSAGE AND
YES, THE DINNER WILL BE FREE

ALEX: I knew you and Ollie were planning something.

ELIZABETH: Well, you know us.

ALEX: I love it, Elizabeth.

ELIZABETH: So, is that a yes?

ALEX: I asked you first.

ELIZABETH: We'll both answer! At the same time. On the count of three —

ALEX: Okay.

ELIZABETH: One —

ALEX: Two —

ELIZABETH: Three —

ALEX & ELIZABETH: Yes!

(Alex and Elizabeth grab each other's hands as the choir behind them sings:)

WHOLE CHOIR: OH MY ALEX!
YOU'RE SAYING YES MADE ME
REALLY SUPER GLAD I TOOK THIS CHANCE
MY HEART IS FULL OF GLEE

ALEX: What were the lyrics if I had said no?

ELIZABETH: I'll tell you later.

(The girls embrace as the lights go down. End of play.)

The Author Speaks

What inspired you to write this play?
I knew right away this was a play I wanted to write! The idea of a promposal was so much fun, and right from the start, I loved the characters in this piece and wanted them to have the prom date of their dreams. Though it's been a long time since I went to prom myself, I remember being really nervous about asking someone, or having them ask me to be their date, and I used this memory to hopefully create a real, believable moment between Elizabeth and Alex as they embarked on this rite of passage together.

Was the structure or other elements of the play influenced by any other work?
I did a more traditional structure for this play, but I did include a musical element (which seems to happen a lot in my work), so that there were opportunities for kids with different talents to be in the show as well. I also thought it was a very true expression of Elizabeth's character to go BIG with her promposal... I don't know that it gets bigger than a show choir.

Have you dealt with the same theme in other works that you have written?
I think this is the first time I've really had an opportunity to explore a lesbian relationship in my work, especially such an important moment like the one these two young women share in *Hashtag Adorable.* At first, I'll admit I was a little daunted. I always worry when I write about experiences outside of my own life that I'm not getting the story right. That because I'm not a lesbian myself, what I write won't accurately capture the experience of a teenage girl coming out to the whole school. In this case, I tried to focus on universal themes (acceptance, anguish over potential heartbreak, and the sweetness of one's

first love), and hope that I got it mostly right. If I'm not right, though, will someone let me know? I'm always open to feedback!

What writers have had the most profound effect on your style?

Amazingly, the writers that have had the most effect on my work are probably not well represented in this kinda straightforward piece. I'm a huge fan of Samuel Beckett, and Sarah Ruhl, but I'm also OBSESSED with *Hamilton* right now. (Who isn't?) Looks like I'll have to wait for my next play to take a stab at a more full-fledged musical.

What do you hope to achieve with this work?

First and foremost, I hope that the actors, director, crew, and audience have FUN! That is always my wish with all of my work. And on a grander scale, I hope that this play shows audiences a relationship that isn't always visible, and by seeing it more often, they'll begin to take it for granted as normal and accepted in their day-to-day lives as well.

What were the biggest challenges involved in the writing of this play?

I might have mentioned this earlier, but I *really* wanted to get this story right and worked for a long time on making sure that the tone, language, and nuance felt natural. I also wanted it to reflect the nervous excitement of this moment for these characters, and have it feel real for the actors playing the roles, as well as the audience watching it.

What are the most common mistakes that occur in productions of your work?

People take their time when the lines can and should be moved through quickly! Actors don't have to worry about relishing the moment in my plays (unless you'd really like to), but I try to write so an actor can say the lines with gusto, energy and humor.

What inspired you to become a playwright?

This is a hard moment to pinpoint because I've been writing "TV Shows" since I was seven (and making my friends act them out on the playground). But I think I started taking it seriously in high school when our spring musical was cancelled. I was doing more acting at the time, and was really bent out of shape that we didn't have ANYTHING to do on stage that semester of my senior year. So, I went home one night with an idea in my head, and wrote a 20-minute musical called *How About That?*. I cast my friends, and convinced our principal to let us put it on—so we did!

I didn't actually get the chance to act like I wanted to, but I think it sealed my fate as a writer/producer for sure. I've been doing it ever since.

What is your writing process?

My process is sort of simple. Once I have an idea, no matter how good or bad it is, I write it down immediately, and as soon as I have time, I write a first draft as quickly as possible (usually in a weekend or so). This is mostly because I know once I have the work on paper, I can start doing edits, revisions, readings for as long as I need, but I can't move forward without doing the heavy lifting of that first draft. Fortunately, I'm pretty impatient, so this strategy works really well for me.

Shakespeare gave advice to the players in *Hamlet*; if you could give advice to your cast what would it be?

Have fun! You have already proven that are so brave by even going on stage that anything you do after that is just icing on the cake. Your audience will love you, your parents and teachers will be so proud of you, and your friends will be in awe (and if they tease you, it's because they only wish they had the courage that you do).

About the Author

Since beginning her career in 2011, **Samantha Macher** has had over 40 productions of her written work both in the U.S. and abroad, and is the winner of a StageSceneLA "Best World Premiere Play" for *War Bride*. Her play *Reset* was a semifinalist for the Princess Grace Playwriting Award, and her award-winning film *Last Pyramid* was accepted into several festivals and has helped in the fundraising and awareness raising efforts for the mission of the Epilepsy Foundation. She has worked in residency with the University of Virginia Drama Department as the Keenan Lecturer, and is working on two new films, *Clown at War* and a screen adaptation of her play *To the New Girl...* Learn more about her at www.samanthamacher.com.

ONE LAST TRICK

A short dramedy by
Anne G'Fellers-Mason

CAST OF CHARACTERS

SYD, a 17-year-old junior, confident in most things, except Claire.

CLAIRE, a 17-year-old junior, confident in all things now.

Magic can't fix everything.

(An open field. A box and a single chair sit beside a table strewn with various magic tricks.)

(SYD leads CLAIRE on slowly. She is blindfolded. He's dressed in a formal suit, she is dressed far more casually.)

CLAIRE: Where are you taking me?

SYD: Just a little further.

CLAIRE: We've walked like three miles.

SYD: Like three feet. Oh, watch your step there.

(She freezes.)

You gotta trust me.

(She takes a comically large step.)

Was that so hard?

CLAIRE: Excruciatingly.

SYD: Pullin' out the fancy SAT words.

(He leads her to the chair.)

Have a seat, m'lady.

(She cautiously feels behind her before sitting.)

CLAIRE: Can I take this off now?

SYD: Not yet. Gimme one second.

CLAIRE: Oh my god!

SYD: Wait for it…wait for it…

(He checks the table quickly to make sure everything's in place. He pulls his phone from his pocket, selects a song, and then re-pockets it. He hurries off.)

CLAIRE: Now?!

SYD: Now!

(Claire takes off the blindfold and looks around.)

What in the—

(Pachelbel's Canon in D begins to play. Syd walks on slowly, making sure his feet touch each time before he moves again.)

CLAIRE: Oh no!

SYD: It's coming back to you, right? The field, the music, the magic?

(He pulls a deck of cards out of nowhere.)

CLAIRE: Oh no!

SYD: The creepy smile, the classical music, the step touch?

(Syd slowly makes his way to the table.)

CLAIRE: Oh, god. The horrors of my eighth birthday party. I worked hard to forget this. This is years of therapy undone.

(Syd begins to perform various magic tricks. He's not that good, but his cheesy grin remains.)

It was so bad. Stop smiling! Stop it! You're freaking me out. Oh, the Pachelbel Magician. I bet he's a serial killer today.

SYD: Don't forget the rhyming.

CLAIRE: No, please, I beg you!

SYD: *(As he performs a trick:)* "Take a card from my deck. Go ahead, give it a check. Put it back, and count to three."

CLAIRE: Worst—birthday—ever.

SYD: "Blink your eyes. Can it be? The card you picked, here on top, for all to see!"

CLAIRE: You brought me out here to relive my nightmares? 'Cause we have this on home video.

SYD: You're gonna love this next trick, I promise.

CLAIRE: The one where he got in the box and disappeared? That was my favorite, yes.

SYD: No, this one!

(Syd pulls flowers out of his sleeve with a note attached to the end. He drops to one knee before Claire. She tentatively accepts the note.)

CLAIRE: "Dearest Claire, will you go to prom with me? I promise all the fun of your eighth birthday, without the creepy magician, only creepy classmates, and hopefully no *Pachelbel's Canon in D*." *(Laughing:)* Yes, a definite yes. I mean, how can anyone resist such a sweet, psychotic smile?

SYD: But wait, there's more.

CLAIRE: More?

(Syd leaves her side and returns to the box. Claire fondly touches the flowers and note.)

You put a lot of thought in this promposal. I hate I missed prom.

SYD: I gotta remember to return that video to your mom.

CLAIRE: You did not?!

SYD: Research, darling.

(He produces a corsage.)

I, uh, picked this out for you. I think it would've gone with that dress you liked.

CLAIRE: Syd, it's beautiful.

(He puts it on her wrist.)

SYD: *(Clearing his throat:)* We'd meet Marcus and Kate for dinner. The menu, Italian, because it's not prom unless you have the absolute dread of getting sauce on your clothes.

CLAIRE: Yum! What would we order?

SYD: Uh, the lady would like the manicotti and I, the chicken parmesan, but you'd make me switch with you.

CLAIRE: Um, yeah, it's what I do.

SYD: Which brings us to, prom!

(He changes the song on his phone to an upbeat dance number. Claire looks out at the field like it's been transformed.)

CLAIRE: Oh, it's beautiful, look at all the carefully crafted papier-mâché decorations.

SYD: First comes the picture.

CLAIRE: Right.

(They strike various poses.)

SYD: I can only afford one, though.

CLAIRE: Cheapskate.

SYD: You're the one who said yes. Next, the awkward fast dancing.

(They dance for a minute, doing various, uncoordinated moves.)

Don't forget the awkward cringing at the dirty dancing couples.

(They cringe in various directions.)

CLAIRE: Someone's gonna be pregnant at graduation. Let's guess who.

SYD & CLAIRE: Valerie!

CLAIRE: Who's the father?

SYD & CLAIRE: Paul!

CLAIRE: Ewwwwww.

SYD: Then the King and Queen are announced.

(They clap sarcastically.)

CLAIRE: What a shocker.

SYD: Super shocked.

CLAIRE: Don't worry, high school's almost over, and the real world is harsh and cold.

SYD: I take comfort in that every night.

CLAIRE: Now what?

(The music switches over to a slow song.)

SYD: Slow songs, you know.

(He fidgets, and she smiles, extending her hand. He accepts her hand, and she pulls him close. They sway, a million unsaid things passing between them.)

CLAIRE: Prom seems like fun. You should go for real next year. You should've gone this year.

SYD: Marcus said it was lame.

CLAIRE: Marcus thinks everything is lame.

SYD: I was studying anyhow —SAT.

CLAIRE: Now *you're* lame.

(They continue to dance.)

Promise me you'll go next year.

SYD: Claire —

CLAIRE: You'll be a senior, you have to go to your senior prom. You should take Stephanie, she thinks you're cute.

SYD: No, I—

CLAIRE: You'll need a whole new promposal, though. Can't do that magician shtick for Stephanie —she'll call the cops.

(Syd stops dancing and takes a step back.)

SYD: *(Exploding:)* I don't wanna go to prom with Stephanie! I wanna go to prom with you! I wanted to last year, and I— I want—

CLAIRE: I know.

SYD: I was gonna ask you, you know, after the dance, to be my girlfriend, because I love you. I've always loved you, Claire.

CLAIRE: Since we were kids, yeah. You're the only one who stayed through the whole magic show fiasco. And that's love, even an eight-year-old knows that.

SYD: I saw how sad you were that day, how disappointed, and I knew then I never wanted to see you sad again. I only wanted to make you smile.

CLAIRE: Hey, I loved my magician promposal. When you do it, it's endearing.

SYD: It wasn't supposed to be this way. We're seventeen! We're supposed to have years!

CLAIRE: Syd—

SYD: *(Brokenly:)* We're young, you were young, that stupid car...

CLAIRE: Syd, stop!

SYD: It's not fair!

(She pulls his head to her shoulders.)

CLAIRE: I know.

(She holds him for a moment.)

You're gonna go to prom next year, maybe not with Stephanie, but somebody. And you'll have an amazing promposal cooked up, and an amazing time at the dance, and an amazing senior year.

(He pulls back and looks at her.)

Thank you, for all this.

SYD: School starts next week and I— I found the video and knew I needed to return it. But I wanted to share this with you, before I did. I wanted you to remember that day as I did.

CLAIRE: I'll think of it as beautiful, always.

(She squeezes his hand.)

SYD: Six months.

CLAIRE: Six months.

SYD: This feels different. I—I've felt you with me since you— you died, but this... Is this goodbye, like, forever?

CLAIRE: I wanted to be sure, you know, that you all were gonna be okay.

(She hugs him one final time.)

And you are, Syd. You're gonna have an amazing life, I promise.

SYD: You would've said yes, right, to the girlfriend thing?

(She nods.)

CLAIRE: Can I finish your magic act for you? There's one last trick.

(She takes the blindfold and ties it around his eyes.)

But you have to trust me.

SYD: Sounds excruciating.

(She turns the music back to "Pachelbel's Canon in D.")

CLAIRE: *(Whispering in his ear:)* Remembering me doesn't mean you can't live your life.

(She kisses his forehead and steps into the box.)

(Reciting from memory:) "Now close your eyes and count to three, and you shall see no more of me."

(Syd slowly counts to three as Claire disappears inside the box. Once he's done, Syd lowers the blindfold and sees that she is gone. He picks up the flowers he gave her and cradles them fondly. With a resolved sigh, he turns off the music. He looks around one last time before taking the flowers with him. It's time to move on.)

(End of play.)

The Author Speaks

What inspired you to write this play?
This play is a spin off from a Theatre for Young Audiences class I took my last summer in the Playwright's Lab at Hollins University. Our class collective had already written a collection of ten-minute plays dealing with parental pressure, and we wanted to funnel that moment into a new theme and a new project. We wanted to tackle the phenomenon of "promposals."

I knew I wanted to take a different approach to my ten-minute offering, and I kept remembering the high school graduation after mine. I went back to watch some of my friends graduate, and a fellow student had passed away in a car wreck earlier that year, and graduation was filled with memories of her. The feeling of connection and sorrow, the mixing of joy and sadness in that room stayed with me, and that's the feeling I wanted to incorporate into *One Last Trick*.

Was the structure or other elements of the play influenced by any other work?
The structure and other elements of the play were not influence by other works, at least that I'm aware of. Of course, there are influences from popular culture when it comes to ghosts staying behind with unfinished business, like the movie *Ghost*, or *Casper* even. There's a long history of this type of story.

Have you dealt with the same theme in other works that you have written?
I've always been fascinated by the supernatural, even if I myself do not really believe in ghosts. I do believe in the possibility, though, and my mother certainly believes herself susceptible to such phenomena. She shared a story about the night her brother died, and how he came to sit on the edge of

her bed and comfort her. I like the idea of being able to provide comfort to those we love after our deaths. It's a nice thought.

What writers have had the most profound effect on your style?
I take a lot of ideas from the works of Tennessee Williams, Arthur Miller, and Paula Vogel. I especially appreciate the way Tennessee Williams mixed comedy with the tragic. I am also inspired by the works of Tom Stoppard and the hope that exists in the tragic moments he captures. Sadness is real, tragedy is real, but so is hope.

What do you hope to achieve with this work?
Dealing with death at a young age is oftentimes harder than dealing with it at an older age. We like to think we're invincible when we're younger, that our friends are invincible, but tragedy can strike at any age. I hope to provide comfort for those who have had to endure such losses, and I want to provide hope that life does go on. Life will be different, but it does go on.

What were the biggest challenges involved in the writing of this play?
The biggest challenge was mixing the humor with the emotion and not letting the piece drown in the sorrow of a tragic, young death. I also wanted it to be a surprise that Claire is dead and not readily apparent to the audience. In a way, this short play works through the five stages of grief in some form or fashion, ending with acceptance at the end. I wanted the audience to come along for that journey through Syd's eyes, and that took some time sitting with the script to achieve.

What are the most common mistakes that occur in productions of your work?
I have to be sure I write in pauses when I want them, otherwise actors do not always deliver the lines with the intent and emotion I want them to have. Sometimes, too, I need an outside reader to remind me I need to work the pauses into the play, because they're in my head, but they do not always translate to the page.

What inspired you to become a playwright?
I have always loved the theatre. I started writing in elementary school, and by middle school I was working on novels. It wasn't until my college career that I tried my hand at writing plays, and I discovered that playwriting is the perfect vehicle to combine my loves of theatre, history, and writing.

How did you research the subject?
The subject is influenced by real life experiences, like the death of my classmate the year after I graduated high school. I lost another friend while I was in high school to a terrible murder, and another friend right after high school to suicide. No one likes to talk about young death, but it happens, and the pain must be dealt with.

What is your writing process?
In the case of this play, I knew I already had the theme: promposal. I also knew I wanted my play to be different, and not the ordinary guy gets girl or vice versa. I wanted a play that used the promposal as a way to deal with a larger issue: the death of a young person. High school seems like it's forever, but it's not, and I wanted my piece to be a reminder of that. There's more to life, to the world, than high school.

Typically, though, I start with an emotion, or idea for a play and build the ground work from there. Like most authors, I recall times in my life when I dealt with similar issues or felt similar emotions and try to bring those moments and feelings to life on the page.

Shakespeare gave advice to the players in *Hamlet*; if you could give advice to your cast what would it be?
Don't be mired down in the sadness of the play. Find the happy, the hope in the words. Do not be afraid to taste the sadness. Do not be afraid to feel it, but be prepared to let it go, to move on. Syd and Claire find their peace through the play. Find yours too.

About the Author

Anne G'Fellers-Mason holds an undergraduate degree in theatre and history from Mars Hill University, a Masters in history from East Tennessee State University, and a Masters in Fine Arts in playwriting from Hollins University. Her one-act, *The War to End All Wars*, received a staged reading at Mars Hill University. Another one-act, *While Sitting in the Park Today*, made it into the semifinals of the National One Act Play competition. Anne works for the Heritage Alliance of Northeast Tennessee and Southwest Virginia in Jonesborough, Tennessee, where she creates original, historical pieces about the history all around her. She travels with her one-woman show, *A Sojourn in Jonesborough*, and her cemetery play, *A Spot on the Hill*, entertains audience members in the Old Jonesborough Cemetery during the cooler months. When she's not writing plays, Anne's busy working on one of her many novels-in-progress.

BANNED FROM STUDENT ACTIVITES

A short comedy by
Adam Hahn

CAST OF CHARACTERS

KATIE, a teenage girl who wants to go to prom.

GRETCHEN, a teenage girl who does not want to go to prom.

(Two teenage girls, KATIE and GRETCHEN, in Katie's room, are sorting a giant pile of clothing, including at least two dresses or long garment bags that could hold dresses.)

GRETCHEN: You can't put that in the donation box. It's a brand new dress.

KATIE: Maybe I should cut it apart and make pillows out of it. That's what they do with bridesmaid dresses, right?

GRETCHEN: You have too many pillows now.

KATIE: You're right. I should burn it.

GRETCHEN: I like fire, but first you should wear it out of the house.

KATIE: Where? The Pie Plate?

GRETCHEN: Yes! Put on the purple dress—

KATIE: It's not purple.

GRETCHEN: Put on that dress, and we'll go to The Pie Plate for mozzarella sticks. You, me, fried cheese?

KATIE: I want fried cheese, but I also want to never be seen in public by anyone ever. Especially in a prom dress.

GRETCHEN: No one will see you.

KATIE: Someone will see me.

GRETCHEN: We'll go right now. The only people at The Pie Plate at four in the afternoon are very old, and they don't know you.

KATIE: Someone will see me.

GRETCHEN: In a town this size? The chance of someone you know seeing you at The Pie Plate in your prom dress is only…

KATIE: Eighty-five percent?

GRETCHEN: Ninety, tops.

KATIE: For the last month of my senior year I'll be the girl who wore her prom dress to The Pie Plate instead of prom.

GRETCHEN: So? It's not like you didn't have a dress in the first place, or you couldn't get a date, or most of the people you find attractive would rather punch you in the face than dance with you.

Katie, you have the ultimate get-out-of-prom-free card.

KATIE: That's not a good thing.

GRETCHEN: It is the best thing. You are BANNED FROM STUDENT ACTIVITIES.

KATIE: How is that good?

GRETCHEN: I'll demonstrate.

And fold your own socks. I'm surprisingly bad with socks.

"What's that, fellow students? You're going to a pep rally and then a football game?"

KATIE: Football season is over.

GRETCHEN: "I won't be there. I'm BANNED FROM STUDENT ACTIVITIES."

KATIE: Nope. Not good. And how can you be bad with socks?

GRETCHEN: Shh, still demonstrating.

"What now? This afternoon we're having a motivational speaker-slash-trumpet player-slash-serious talk about abstinence? Have fun! I'll be in the library with the other students BANNED FROM STUDENT ACTIVITIES."

KATIE: Still bad. Angry teachers. Yelling parents. The trumpet guy talked about abstinence?

GRETCHEN: Using his trumpet as a metaphor.

KATIE: I thought they weren't going to have any more abstinence speakers after the last one.

GRETCHEN: There will always be abstinence speakers. There just won't be open Q and A afterward.

Speaking of the infamous hot dog question, was Cody in the library with you?

KATIE: No, I think he has to go to the counseling office during assemblies.

GRETCHEN: Wow, that's like Banned from Student Activities solitary confinement. He'll never have to go to another pep rally, and he's a sophomore.

KATIE: I place this jacket in the donation box in his honor. It looks the way he smells.

GRETCHEN: I should have asked the hot dog question. I've been trying to get banned from student activities for twelve years. It's like they know making me go to things is the worst punishment they have.

KATIE: They should make you go to prom.

GRETCHEN: That would be cruel and unusual.

KATIE: I've got a dress you can borrow.

GRETCHEN: That's yours.

KATIE: You should try it on.

GRETCHEN: I'd mess it up. I'd get it dirty or something.

KATIE: It would look good on you.

GRETCHEN: Of course it would. I'm gorgeous.

But you picked it out. You should get to wear it at least once. You'll look really great.

KATIE: Thank you.

GRETCHEN: Better than you ever did in these pants.

KATIE: Donation box. If you see the matching vest, put it in the trash.

GRETCHEN: Thanks for standing up for me.

KATIE: You would have done the same thing for me.

GRETCHEN: I'll never have to. No one's ever going to shove you out of a bathroom. The whole school is in love with you. You got banned from prom, and you're still invited to every after-party.

Everybody hates me. I get shoved around enough that I'm used to it, and you got in a slap-fight to stop it. Thanks.

KATIE: Forget about it. Are they leaving you alone now?

GRETCHEN: Of course not, because violence never solves anything.

KATIE: Especially if you fight as badly as I do.

GRETCHEN: You made a good effort, although for a slap-fight there wasn't much slapping or fighting.

KATIE: Just enough to keep me home on prom night.

GRETCHEN: Home? You're still going out tomorrow, aren't you?

KATIE: Where, The Pie Plate?

GRETCHEN: No, somewhere good. Where's Jason taking you for dinner?

KATIE: We didn't talk about it.

GRETCHEN: You should go to MacIntyre's downtown.

KATIE: A lot of people are going to MacIntyre's. Remember, I don't want to be seen by anyone, especially on prom night.

GRETCHEN: Everyone's going early, before the dance. You two go later, when it's quiet. Get that chocolate cake that takes forever, and then you can decide if there are any after-parties you could stand to be seen at.

KATIE: That sounds nice.

GRETCHEN: And you can wear the dress! Does Jason still have his tux reserved?

KATIE: We haven't talked about it.

GRETCHEN: Talk to him. Tell him he needs to bring you a corsage.

KATIE: I don't know if I'll see him this weekend.

GRETCHEN: Why wouldn't you? You have a date.

KATIE: I don't know.

GRETCHEN: He asked you to go to prom with him. Now he has to not go to prom with you.

KATIE: The thing is, he never asked me.

GRETCHEN: But you've been dating all year.

KATIE: I know.

GRETCHEN: And it's prom!

KATIE: I know.

GRETCHEN: And you helped him pick out a tux?

KATIE: Yes I did.

GRETCHEN: And three months ago you told him, "I'm driving to Cedar Rapids to buy this not-purple prom dress, and I can't return it later because the store is closing." Right?

KATIE: Right, but we never figured out how he was going to ask me.

GRETCHEN: How is that difficult?

KATIE: He was going to ask me at The Dairy Cone, because that's where we went on our first date, but we had to wait for it to open for the summer. Then it didn't open on schedule —

GRETCHEN: Because of the asbestos.

KATIE: Then it didn't open at all —

GRETCHEN: Because of the plague rats.

KATIE: That was just a rumor. They were normal rats.

GRETCHEN: But still not romantic rats.

KATIE: Finally, Jason's brother brought ice cream from the Dairy Cone in Muscatine, but it melted. He was trying to re-freeze it when I got Banned from Student Activities.

So he never actually asked me.

GRETCHEN: But it's not like he has other plans. He isn't going to prom without you.

KATIE: I don't know. He can if he wants to.

GRETCHEN: Have you talked to him at all since the slap-fight?

KATIE: We talked that night.

GRETCHEN: And?

KATIE: And I don't think we want to go to prom together.

GRETCHEN: Did you break up?

KATIE: I guess so.

GRETCHEN: Three days ago?

KATIE: Yeah.

GRETCHEN: And I'm hearing about this now?

KATIE: This is the first time it came up.

GRETCHEN: Oh.

KATIE: What?

GRETCHEN: That's why this giant pile of clothing seemed so familiar.

KATIE: I don't know what you mean.

GRETCHEN: Katie, do you remember freshman year when Tyler Duffy broke up with you because you didn't go to his basketball game, and that was all we talked about for all of Thanksgiving break?

KATIE: Yes.

GRETCHEN: Do you remember seventh grade? Josh Ritter lied about sitting next to Sarah Tonk on the bus, and I avoided you for two weeks because I couldn't hear about it one more time without stabbing myself in the eardrums?

KATIE: Yes.

GRETCHEN: Do you remember the four times you've broken up with guys over things they said about me, and then you didn't want to talk about it at all?

KATIE: Yes.

GRETCHEN: You just wanted to go home, do laundry, and throw away a bunch of your clothes?

KATIE: It's always a good time to get rid of junk you don't need.

GRETCHEN: What did Jason say?

KATIE: It doesn't matter.

GRETCHEN: I've probably heard it before. Maybe he doesn't know why you got in a fight for me. Maybe he doesn't think people like me should be allowed in the bathroom at all.

KATIE: Something like that.

GRETCHEN: Thanks for standing up for me again.

KATIE: It's not your fault I had to. It's his. I don't want to go to MacIntyre's with him if he thinks about you that way.

Maybe I shouldn't have slapped Jen, but everybody knows you get shoved around all the time, and nobody does anything about it. I don't want to go to any after-parties with people who were allowed to go to prom because they didn't stand up for you.

It's just prom. In ten years, no one's going to remember. Who cares?

GRETCHEN: You do. It's killing you that you can't go.

KATIE: Obviously! I just threw away all of my pillowcases. How am I going to cover my pillows?

GRETCHEN: And you deserve to go.

Katherine? Will you not go to prom with me?

KATIE: What?

GRETCHEN: Will you put on that dress tomorrow? I'll pick you up, I'll bring the corsage Jason should have given you, and I'll take you out to dinner.

KATIE: At The Pie Plate?

GRETCHEN: No, somewhere far away, where no one knows us. The Pie Plate in Galesburg.

KATIE: Mozzarella sticks?

GRETCHEN: With extra red sauce. We'll stay until they stop refilling our drinks, and then we'll come here and watch bad movies.

And ten years from now... You'll be at the class reunion. Everyone is still going to love you, and no one is going to remember you weren't at prom. And I'll be somewhere else, because I never want to see those people again.

But I'm going to remember my prom night, because I was with my best friend, who got banned from student activities when she stood up for me.

Katherine, will you not go to prom with me?

KATIE: Yes.

GRETCHEN: You have made me the happiest miserable high school lesbian in the entire American Midwest.

KATIE: What are you going to wear?

GRETCHEN: I don't know. This? All my clothes look the same.

KATIE: You're dressing up.

GRETCHEN: I could borrow a necktie?

KATIE: You'd look good in my homecoming dress from the fall.

GRETCHEN: I'd look amazing. I'm gorgeous.

KATIE: Gretchen, will you put on a fancy dress and not go to prom with me?

GRETCHEN: Yes.

KATIE: Thanks for making this fun.

GRETCHEN: You would have done the same thing for me.

(End of play.)

The Author Speaks

What inspired you to write this play?
I remember being in high school and not wanting to attend prom. I hated the idea of renting a tux, going to eat somewhere "fancy," then voluntarily spending Saturday night with hundreds of my classmates. I was much happier watching bad movies in a basement with two or three friends, or occupying a table in one of the few restaurants that would let you order a plate of fries and keep refilling your Cherry Coke for three hours. My best friend at the time was very different: she knew everyone's name, enjoyed student activities, would take any excuse to dress up, and loved going to dances. We were opposites in many ways, but I remember that friendship being one of the best parts of high school.

What do you hope to achieve with this work?
I want to honestly depict high school as an institution that is terrible, for at least a day, for everyone who attends. (I say that looking back on my own high school experience, which was, on the balance, pretty good.) I want to show two teenagers going through a terrible time without being crushed by it: they don't think it's their fault that things are terrible, they don't think things are always going to be terrible, and they're not lashing out at others. Two of my favorite lines are the times that Gretchen states matter-of-factly that she is gorgeous. No matter how she's been treated at school, she has kept a sense of her own self-worth. Most importantly, this script is about the value of friendship and the importance of caring for each other.

What inspired you to become a playwright?
The short answer is that all humans are born storytellers, and writing a play is usually the best way to tell the stories I want to tell.

Working on this script in particular, I'm reminded of the time I spent in high school and college reading, attending theatre, watching movies, competing in and judging speech and debate tournaments, and acting. I think there are two primary ways that writers are motivated by the work of others. The first is putting down a book or walking out of a play thinking, "That was terrible! I could write something better, and no one will have to sit through this garbage again." The second is enjoying something and thinking, "This is great! If I write something really good, someone else will enjoy it as much as I'm enjoying this right now!" My growth into playwriting came more from the second type of motivation, and with every script I hope that if I get the words right actors and audiences will enjoy the stories I wrote. (Then they'll write something even better, and I'll get to be inspired by that.)

Are any characters modeled after real life or historical figures?
This is loosely based on my own high school experience. *Very* loosely. I was never actually a bullied lesbian. The towns named in the script are close to where I grew up, and the restaurants are based on places I ate. I should make it clear that as far as I know the ice cream stands in my hometown never had a rat problem. The mozzarella sticks are real, as are friends just as good as Katie and Gretchen.

What is your writing process?
My process varies quite a bit depending on the project. There are some ideas I want to get on paper as soon as I can, and others need to ferment in the back of my head for a year or more before I get a handle on how to write them. Longer projects tend to take a lot more planning and outlining. I always like to block off the time to bang out a first draft in as few sittings as possible. On a project the size of *Banned from Student Activities*, I feel ready to write when I have a few too

many ideas to fit into the script. In the first draft, I knew where I had to get at the ending, there were a few things I absolutely had to explain along the way, and I had a relatively short time to cover those and enjoy letting Katie and Gretchen talk. Knowing extra pieces of backstory or topics they could have bantered about meant that at every beat I could choose an interesting or revealing way to move toward the next piece of information. (Maybe someday I'll write the other version, where Katie relates everything to Jane Austen novels and Gretchen relates everything to horror films.)

About the Author

Adam Hahn is a resident playwright of SkyPilot Theatre Company in Los Angeles. SkyPilot has produced several of his plays, including *Overlay*, *The Mermaid Wars*, *KONG: A Goddamn Thirty-Foot Gorilla*, and *Earthbound*, a sci-fi musical written with composer Jonathan Price and lyricist Chana Wise. Some of his plays for young audiences are available from YouthPLAYS. Adam holds an MFA in playwriting from the Playwright's Lab at Hollins University. He is also an occasional actor and graduated from the improv training program at at iO West.

PROM NINJA

A short comedy by
Nicole B. Adkins

CAST OF CHARACTERS

NINA, female, a high school senior. Focused, skeptical, probably valedictorian.

COLBY, female, a high school senior. Self-obsessed.

JUSTIN, male, a high school senior. Trying to muster the courage to prompose.

SERGIO, male, a high school freshman. Shirtless romantic.

(NINA, a high school senior, is sitting at Taco Shack on her free period, working on her computer. She is visibly annoyed. After a moment, JUSTIN enters wearing his backpack. Nervous and a little sweaty, he is dressed in a shirt, tie, and black slacks.)

NINA: Where have you been!? Woah... You smell like you had a fight with a can of air freshener. Why the...? *(Gestures to his clothing:)* You look uncomfortable.

JUSTIN: OK, so prom is in 5 days and —

NINA: *(Shudders.)* Ugh. Not you too. Apparently I've overestimated you all these years. I didn't think Colby was your type —

JUSTIN: No — wait —

NINA: And what a choice of a romantic venue! Taco Shack. Not to mention we are supposed to be working —

JUSTIN: Look, we're running out of time —

NINA: Yeah! I know! Why can't anybody focus!? Prom season hits and everybody's reduced to a giant walking hormone —

JUSTIN: Nina! I've been trying to work up the nerve —

(COLBY enters, sashaying.)

COLBY: OMG! You guys are so not going to believe this. Sergio has uploaded another video!

NINA: Nice of you to show up, Colby.

COLBY: I had *things* to do. Now, watch.

NINA: No.

COLBY: But — this is like, breaking news!

NINA: Please google the definition of news. This is just some fame-hungry freshman trying to get himself invited to prom.

COLBY: Just watch.

(Colby gets close to show them her phone.)

JUSTIN: Gotta give the guy credit. He has no fear.

COLBY: Mmm, Justin, don't you smell and look nice. Did you have something special planned today?

JUSTIN: Uh...

NINA: UGH!! Don't make me throw up. Can we please get to work?? You two can make out or whatever after we're done and I'm gone!

JUSTIN: I'm not — that's not —

COLBY: *(Watching the video:)* You know, he's kinda cute for a noodle-armed little geek. *(Beat. They stare at her.)* What? I mean, his name is *Sergio!* It's like a romance novel waiting to happen. You know, in a year or five.

NINA: That's probably not even his real name. *(Colby sticks out her tongue.)* Look, we are running out of time —

COLBY: I know. Things are getting ridiculous. I mean — *me? With no date!?* It's like the world's inside-out or something. You should see my dress. *(Leans against Justin.)* It hugs in all the right places, with a super low neck — *(She pulls her collar down to expose some cleavage.)* And yet, I am still waiting for the right man to ask me...

NINA: Man! Man?? I can't even. Ugh!! Earth to Justin! If you could stop staring at her chest please for a minute so we can concentrate on planning the photo layout? And we still need a topic!!

(He is mesmerized by cleavage. Nina smacks him.)

JUSTIN: *(Snapping out of it:)* Sorry! Boobs! Involuntary!

COLBY: Let's just watch this one video and then I swear we'll concentrate.

NINA: And you, *Editor-in-Chief!* I wish you'd take your job seriously. It's always like you'd rather be getting a manicure.

COLBY: *Well...*

NINA: There are people who would love your title, you know. People who don't have your family's money. People who actually have to *earn* their way into college.

COLBY: Oh, like you don't have scholarships to everywhere.

JUSTIN: *(He's watching his phone, we hear cheesy romantic music.)* OK, this is kind of awesome.

NINA: Seriously?! Justin!

> *(Colby leans in. Nina, throwing in the towel, looks on with them. SERGIO, a freshman, appears elsewhere on stage, shirtless, with a rose in his teeth. He does not have romance-novel muscles. He has an Italian accent. He is wearing rollerblades, though not adroitly. He could fall at any minute. If a fan could be blowing his hair that would be ideal.)*

SERGIO: Let her get one look at these muscles, and she will not resist this man-hunk!

COLBY: Ha! This kid is epic!

JUSTIN: I gotta say. I wish I had his confidence.

SERGIO: Any lady would be lucky to have Sergio.

NINA: Um, since when can freshmen leave campus? And where did he get that ridiculous accent?? I bet he's actually from Kansas or something.

COLBY: Whatever. He has an accent. And look how many followers he has. *Every*body is watching this. Now shhh!

SERGIO: Lucky lady, I am headed your way. I know you watch me on the video screen because who could tear their eyes away? I will ride to you on a white horse, or in the

absence of a white horse which I do not have, I will glide to
you on my roller shoes —

> *(He glides on his rollerblades and attempts to execute some
> smooth maneuver. He is not successful. He barely saves himself
> from falling. He comes close to the audience, leans in.)*

I am rolling your way. Soon I will be to you and ask you to
prom on my video screen while our fans watch on dreaming
of the romance. I will carry you to prom on my white horse or
in the absence of a white horse which I do not have, you could
drive us, la mia tesora!

COLBY: And he speaks Italian!

JUSTIN: Yeah man. I should take lessons.

NINA: He knows a few words! He probably got them off the
internet!

SERGIO: I sign off for now, la mia piccola tigre! I am only
some short minutes from your destination. I am skipping the
school to find you since after I did the spy work to find out
where you would be at this very hour! I have rolled so far...
Ciao for just a little moments mia dulce.

> *(He skates off, barely managing not to fall.)*

NINA: Skipping! See? I bet he gets expelled.

JUSTIN: It's kind of inspiring. I wish I had his guts.

COLBY: *(Flirting:)* You should just get them. And then decide
who you're promposing to, Justin.

NINA: If you really want a career as a journalist, you might
want to work on your grammar. "To whom you are
promposing" would be correct. If promposing were even
actually a word. Which it isn't.

> *(They stare at her.)*

COLBY: Are you even *planning* to go to prom?

NINA: Obviously I have to! Who else is going to finish the yearbook spread?! But I'm not bringing a date. I probably won't even dress up. I'll wear black and hide in the shadows.

COLBY: OK, weirdo. Like you wouldn't draw attention to yourself *that* way.

JUSTIN: Everybody would be like, who invited the ninja?

COLBY: *(Laughing too hard:)* You are *so* funny.

JUSTIN: Uh…thanks? Seriously though. I'm glad you're planning to go…

COLBY: OMG guys. Speaking of going to prom. I *know* I've had plenty of chances, but I was totally keeping my options open. Now it's pretty much countdown, and— *(Batting her eyelashes at Justin:)* there are only a couple people I'd consider saying yes to…

NINA: To WHOM I'D CONSIDER SAYING YES!

COLBY & JUSTIN: Huh?

NINA: Would you two PLEASE stop flirting and help me! Our free period is almost over and we haven't accomplished anything!!

JUSTIN: There's another video.

COLBY: We *have* to watch.

NINA: You two go ahead. *I'm* going to work.

JUSTIN: *(We hear cheesy music again.)* Wow…

COLBY: What?! What's he doing now?

> *(She leans into Justin, flirtatiously. Sergio enters on his rollerblades. He is exhausted. He stops to catch his breath. Then he leans into the audience, stage whispering.)*

SERGIO: I am right outside the building where you are, luce mia! I rolled here with all of my gusto since I am not yet old enough to have a vehicle!

NINA: "*I am not yet...*" Proper usage of prepositions! He actually has a better command of the English language than *some* people I know.

COLBY: Rude.

SERGIO: I must to stay quiet for the moment so as to build the suspense! The sign says I am not allowed in without my shirt, and I do not know how they feel about the rolling shoes! But I do not care! I do anything for amore! I will catch my breath and adjust my hair in the reflection of a car window and then I am coming to give you my heart and wet kisses!

(He skates off.)

JUSTIN: I gotta say, the guy just puts himself right out there.

COLBY: You could do that too. You just need to figure out a super romantic and awesome way to ask the right girl.

JUSTIN: *(Sarcastic:)* Yeah, easier than it sounds, right?

NINA: *(Beat, staring at Justin's phone:)* You, know...maybe there's a story here.

COLBY: What, like *actual news?* Told you!

NINA: No, I mean... This "promposal" thing. It's so much pressure. But on the other hand it's also...kind of freeing. I don't really see the point of it since we are all just in high school and it's not like this silly dance really means anything in the grand scheme of things—

COLBY: Total wet blanket. Every time.

NINA: But, I mean, all we have is *now*, right? No matter where we go, what we do with our lives in the future, right now THIS is the moment we are experiencing. This is our moment.

COLBY: I don't get it.

JUSTIN: I think you're on to something...

NINA: There are things we can do that are really stupid. Things that can haunt us — like if we flunk algebra or do something really awful to somebody — and then there are things we *think* will haunt us, but maybe that's just us moving out of our comfort zone?

COLBY: You are totally rambling.

NINA: What I mean is, whether I go or not. Whether this whole thing is just a chauvinistic marketing scheme dreamed up by the formal wear and flower industries. Whether Sergio's target says yes — or if he actually escaped from a loony bin. Or whether Colby finds the perfect date — or Justin gets up the nerve to ask her —

JUSTIN: But I —

COLBY: Right?!

NINA: What MATTERS...is that we don't have regrets. That we don't let fear stop us from taking risks! *That* matters. That is a premise I can write a story around. *(Beat.)* I mean, *around which* I can write...whatever.

(She gets to work typing, excited, oblivious to anything else.)

JUSTIN: *(Epiphany:)* Yeah...you're...right!! I'll be back in a minute!

(He exits, excited.)

COLBY: I think he's finally going to ask me!! How do I look? *(Takes a selfie blowing a kiss to herself.)* Ooh! His eyes will SO match my dress! I totally thought about going with Anthony but he was too tall. Justin and I will look way better in pics.

NINA: *(Shocked out of writing:)* THAT'S why you want to go with him?

COLBY: I mean, I've GOT to get a date ASAP and he's my best last choice.

NINA: Are you serious??

(Beat, Colby shrugs.)

He is the nicest, coolest, funniest guy who has *ever* liked you — and *if* you are *lucky* enough for him to ask you —

COLBY: OMG. You *are* jealous.

NINA: I am not! Justin and I are just friends! We've been friends since kindergarten! Ever since he helped me learn to tie my shoes and I—I... *(Epiphany:)* I...like him. I *like* like him! And I *am* jealous, but mostly because...you don't deserve him! And I'm not going to let you ruin his senior prom! Not without a fight.

(Nina runs her fingers through her hair, stands up, smooths her clothes.)

COLBY: What. Are. You. *Doing?*

NINA: No regrets!

(Nina starts typing something new on her computer. Colby looks over Nina's shoulder.)

COLBY: You've got to be kidding me! You versus me? Good luck.

(We hear cheesy romance music from Colby's phone.)

Oooh! Hold up! New video!

(Colby tunes in. Nina continues to type. Sergio skates on.)

SERGIO: I am opening the door, I am...here! I am going to ask you for all the world to see!

(Sergio puts the rose between his teeth. Holding his phone out to take footage of the whole scene, he skates into Nina and Colby's space. He gets down on one knee beside their table.)

COLBY: Oh my gosh, another promposal!!!

SERGIO: Amore mia, you and me, we would make beautiful bambinos! Someday! But first we should go to the prom! Please, Nina, will you do me the honor?

COLBY: *Nina??*

NINA: Whaaaa—??

COLBY: *WHY??*

SERGIO: Smart is sexy, no? And everybody say she is going to be valedictoria!

COLBY: *(Grabs at his phone:)* Turn that off right now!

(Justin enters, carrying a tray.)

JUSTIN: Woah, Sergio! Asking Colby? Good for you!

SERGIO: Scusi? No, I—

JUSTIN: Look, I'm sorry, this isn't the most romantic idea I've ever had—or the most romantic locale as you pointed out—but the thing is I've been trying to get up the nerve and come up with a perfect idea for weeks, trust me—and I know you've already eaten lunch...but what you said just a minute ago inspired me and I didn't want to let the moment pass so—just—just look at this tray and then please tell me yes.

(He gets on one knee, presenting a rather crushed corsage from his backpack to Nina. Colby and Nina, both dumbfounded, look at the tray.)

COLBY: Did you write *"Prom"* with a question mark in *refried beans?!*

JUSTIN: There's surprisingly little to work with at the Taco Shack. Anyway, it's dumb, I know. But I couldn't lose my chance, Nina —

NINA: Justin.

(Nina turns her lap-top to Justin. It has a picture of Nina and Justin and says "Justin, will you go to prom with me?")

JUSTIN: *(Reads:)* Will you...go to prom with me!? *(Huge grin.)* Does it really say...?

(Nina smiles. She and Justin stare into each other's eyes.)

COLBY: This isn't happening.

(Sergio skates around Justin and Nina.)

SERGIO: *(To Justin:)* I challenge you to a duel!

COLBY: *(To Nina:)* Backstabber!!

SERGIO: No! I have honor! We will fight to the face!

JUSTIN: Sorry Colby, but it was always...only, *ever* about Nina.

(Colby grabs Sergio's phone, turns it off, and sits on it.)

COLBY: I told you to turn that off!

SERGIO: Hey!

(Sergio tries to get his phone back, to no avail.)

Ohhh! I will die for love!

(He clutches his heart.)

NINA: *(Smiles, to Sergio:)* Thanks for thinking of me, but I doubt you'll die.

JUSTIN: You'll be fine, man. You're a really brave dude.

(Sergio stands, complimented.)

SERGIO: Si I am, no?

(He takes back his phone; Colby doesn't put up a fight.)

NINA: *(To Colby:)* Hey — you OK?

COLBY: Yeah... I, uh... It's just... I...didn't really get any other promposals.

NINA: *Whaaa...? None?* But I thought —

COLBY: I started that rumor. Thought maybe it would drive up demand or something. *(To Sergio:)* Tell a soul and I'll destroy you.

SERGIO: *(Considering Colby:)* Fierce. Yet vulnerable...

NINA: Wow, I'm sorry Colby. I thought —

COLBY: I know. Everybody did. It's cool. I'm...happy for you guys or whatever.

JUSTIN: Thank you.

NINA: I'm sure somebody will ask you. I mean — you're *Colby Jones!*

COLBY: I think everybody's intimidated by my looks or power or something.

NINA: *(Beat.)* Um, yeah. That's probably it. *(Looks at her phone:)* Oh my gosh. So sorry, but I'm gonna be late! I've got to go write a story.

(Justin takes her hand and smiles at her.)

And find a dress.

JUSTIN: *(Smiling:)* Or we could go as ninjas.

NINA: Seriously? THAT would be amazing.

(Nina begins to pack up her stuff. Justin helps. To Colby:)

You gonna be OK?

COLBY: Don't worry about me.

(Nina and Justin exit holding hands.)

(Takes a deep breath.) No regrets... *(To Sergio:)* Um... So... Do you, like, wanna go with me or something? To prom, I mean. I'd have to, like, take you shopping first, and —

SERGIO: Scusi?

COLBY: Nevermind, that was dumb, I was just kidding — *(Trying not to cry:)* I gotta get out of here —

SERGIO: There, there, scary, beautiful cheerleading model type which has never before been at all my flavor —

COLBY: Excuse me?

SERGIO: I am seeing — a whole new side to your kind, no?

(He tilts his phone slightly, begins to record again surreptitiously. Getting on one knee, he puts the rose in his mouth.)

Mia luce! Beautiful one, since you ask so romantically, I would love to go to the prom with you.

COLBY: Wait — Are you recording again?? Stop it! Give me that!

SERGIO: For some kisses, I will consider your demand!

COLBY: You better turn that thing off or you won't live 'til prom!

SERGIO: Oh, *merindina!* The thrill of the chase! Life is so good!

(She chases him offstage. End of play.)

The Author Speaks

What inspired you to write this play?
While teaching a Writing for Young Audiences class at Hollins University for their MFA Playwriting program, I had a student who happened to be a high school drama teacher. He regaled us with outstanding stories of contemporary young romantics/hopefuls "promposing" to each other in truly epic ways. This of course launched a class-wide YouTube-watching frenzy of teen flashmobs, airplane writing escapades, backyard ninja candlelit serenades, and other impressive endeavors, as well as article-reading and plenty of informal surveying of teens on the front lines. A handful of us felt that this movement deserved further theatrical investigation. We decided to create a collection of short plays, and ultimately invited a number of professional playwrights outside of the class to contribute to it as well. I got to thinking about how I would have felt as a teenager about promposals. I remember that inviting people, or getting invited to dances was of course a HUGE deal, but nothing compared to today's high stakes — where open-source media has created the potential of one's promposal successes or failures being launched onto the national stage. The excitement of all this, but also the immense pressure (not to mention the strong cynicism I would have felt), inspired me to create a piece in which these themes are at play.

Have you dealt with the same theme in other works that you have written?
I often write about characters who are deciding who they are and who they want to become. In this particular piece, Nina, being an intelligent and driven person with her eyes on the future, is naturally skeptical of what she sees as the senseless high school social scene. She also, however, really does want to fulfill the role she feels she should embody: that of a

balanced and impartial journalist. Furthermore, she can't help being at least somewhat caught up in her current reality. Therefore, she has to decide how to approach a big moment in her high school career (both social and academic), even when her first inclination is to write it all off.

What writers have had the most profound effect on your style?
I have always been a voracious reader. As a kid I spent years reading all the myths, legends, and original fairy tales I could find. I moved from there to authors who explore the mythic and fantastical in their writing (often fantasy or sci-fi), such as George MacDonald, Hans Christian Andersen, Ursula K. LeGuin, Madeleine L'Engle, C.S. Lewis, Lois Lowry, Orson Scott Card and Ray Bradbury. I also loved authors of classic books with strong female characters, such as Jane Austen and L.M. Montgomery. I was also very strongly affected by my years working as an actor in theatre for young audiences and was amazed to discover the work of playwrights like Suzan Zeder and José Cruz González and to get to perform in plays like *The Yellow Boat* by David Saar.

What do you hope to achieve with this work?
My purpose as a writer is always to entertain and to tell a good story, foster empathy, and make individuals feel heard/understood. If I have amused and/or challenged audience members and actors, I'll be happy. Better yet, if I have been able to connect with their fears or dreams, or helped someone to articulate her or his feelings about the excitement, stress, meaning (or lack-thereof) of prom and/or promposing, I'll be delighted.

What were the biggest challenges involved in the writing of this play?
With a short play, it is vital that each character be given the room to be as nuanced as possible. This is also true with a

longer play, but it is inherently one of the biggest challenges of more compressed work. Because this collection explores a subject with inbuilt high stakes for everyone involved, it seemed important to me that I pay homage to several unique perspectives in my piece. I wanted each character to have their triumphant as well as vulnerable moments, without bogging down the tempo or killing the comedy. Getting the ending just right with Colby and Sergio was the most challenging part. I wanted for us get a glimpse of the "real" Colby, and also felt Sergio's ambitious efforts deserved some reward.

What are the most common mistakes that occur in productions of your work?

I love to explore the use of subtext. Because subtext is not always obvious, sometimes ideas and feelings get missed in performance. This can be as much my fault as that of the actors or director—it is always a learning process for me how much I should say and how much I should simply let actors and directors discover on their own. I would encourage actors in any play (not just mine) to really delve into every character's goals and motivations, and try to find what makes them say and do the things they do. This said, sometimes reinterpretations work in my favor, as an actor or director may discover an idea or feeling I didn't even know was there, and give the line a much better reading than I had even imagined! Either way, when a producing company and its members do their homework, it always shows.

Also, I love physicality and "impossible" theatrical moments. These work best when the producing company takes fun risks and meets my imagination with theirs.

Finally, related to the idea of producing companies doing their homework: in this specific piece, Sergio is definitely a "larger-than-life" character. I would urge actors in this role to really think about what Sergio wants and what makes him tick, so as to avoid the obvious and easy choice of playing him as simply a cartoon or caricature. While comic timing and pace are really important where he is concerned, so are honesty and believability. The same could be said, to a degree, of Colby.

What inspired you to become a playwright?

My father had his undergraduate degree in theatre and owned a video production company through my childhood. My mother was always a poet and a writer, and ran the production company with my dad, writing many of the scripts for commercials, how-to-videos and other jobs. Subsequently, I spent a lot of time on set, either just hanging around or being thrown into projects as a handy, free actor. I also participated in theatre from a very early age. (My first appearance on stage was as the dove in *Godspell*... If you know the show, there is no dove. I spent most of the show scratching my tights). Anyway, that infamous theatre bug...it bit me. I acted, consumed theatre, read every book I could find, and wrote stories and plays from a very early age. Given the combination of my parents' talents, my great respect for both of them, and my love of theatre and literature, being a playwright kind of felt inevitable. Though I began as an actor and that influences every play I write, I became far more entranced by creating and peopling entire worlds than actually being onstage myself. I love to try and create worlds and characters that actors, designers, and directors might enjoy bringing to life, and to see what new colors and depth they bring to my initial envisioning.

How did you research the subject?

As mentioned above, a playwriting student of mine first introduced me to the magical world of promposing, and provided a great number of fabulous stories witnessed first-hand. Lots of additional articles, surveying of teens I know, as well as endless YouTube videos helped to fill out my "promposal-cation."

What is your writing process?
It is a bit different for every play, but it usually involves initial research, then planning and loose outlining, more research, all followed by a massive, coffee-dependent, snack-consuming writing binge. Though they are nearly impossible to find (especially as a mom), I covet big unstructured chunks of time in which to play with my characters in their world. Next, I usually take a bit of distance — hours, days, sometimes weeks, depending on deadlines — followed by another big rewriting/editing binge.

I like to move around a lot while writing, getting a feel for each character's physical self, and reading lines out-loud in character voices. Basically, I spend masses of time dancing around my computer, talking in weird voices, looking like a total loony-toon.

After I have a draft I feel is ready for scrutiny, I put together a reading with respondents and actors so I can hear it aloud (followed by more bizarre computer dances and muttering).

Shakespeare gave advice to the players in *Hamlet*; if you could give advice to your cast what would it be?
Figure out what the characters want. Find and explore the different ways they go about getting what they want. Be fearless.

About the Author

Nicole B. Adkins has taught classes and workshops to students of various ages at theatres, K-12 schools, and universities. Her plays have been performed at Children's Theatre of Charlotte, Hollins University, Mill Mountain

Theatre, Studio Roanoke, Creative Drama Children's Theatre in Winston-Salem (NC), SkyPilot Theatre in Los Angeles, the American International School in Guangzhou (China), and other theatres, schools, and museums nationally and abroad. She has six plays published through YouthPLAYS, where she also serves as Artistic Associate. She collaborated with Matt Omasta of Utah State University on a book entitled *Playwriting and Young Audiences: Collected Wisdom and Practical Advice from the Field* (Intellect Press, 2017). National playwriting awards include the Waldo M. and Grace C. Bonderman Award and recognition in the Beverly Hills Theatre Guild Marilyn Hall competition. A Hollins Children's Literature MFA graduate and Playwright's Lab Core Faculty member, Nicole is also a member of Dramatists Guild and TYA/USA.

THE CLARINET SECTION IS SICK OF YOUR GARBAGE

A short comedy by
Megan Gogerty

CAST OF CHARACTERS

CHELSEA, a teen girl, smart.

JILL, a teen girl, snarky.

BETHANY, a teen girl, sweet.

JENNA, a teen girl, revolutionary.

(Three clarinet players, CHELSEA, JILL and BETHANY, eating lunch outside the band room.)

CHELSEA: *(Standing with importance:)* I would just like to point out for the record —

JILL: *(Throwing bits of sandwich at her:)* Boo!

BETHANY: No proclamations, please!

CHELSEA: — That not only is the concept of prom inherently fascist — institutionally sanctioned fun, anyone? No, thank you — But that the promposal —

BETHANY: We know what you think, everybody knows what you think.

CHELSEA: *(Undeterred:)* — The promposal is particularly ridiculous because it's humiliating, sexist, classist —

JILL: If you say "consumerist," I get your Doritos.

CHELSEA: Well, it is.

JILL: Is what?

CHELSEA: Consumerist.

(Jill snatches the Doritos from Chelsea.)

BETHANY: Sit down, Chelsea. It's none of our business.

CHELSEA: I just wanted it stated for the record.

BETHANY: Jenna's choices are her own to make.

CHELSEA: Jenna is going to make an idiot of herself for nothing.

BETHANY: Maybe. You don't know.

CHELSEA: It's one thing to make an idiot of yourself if you have a good reason.

JILL: You would know, Chelsea.

CHELSEA: He's going to say no. She's going to be humiliated, and he's going to say no.

BETHANY: He might say yes.

CHELSEA: He's a trumpet player.

BETHANY: I know.

CHELSEA: *(To Jill:)* Are you seriously going to keep my Doritos?

JILL: *(Reluctantly surrenders Doritos.)* All trumpet players are cocky and arrogant. She should've asked somebody in the low brass section.

BETHANY: Oh, please. Nobody's that desperate.

JILL: At least they would have said yes! She wants to go to prom. You think any of them have dates?

BETHANY: Then she would've had to get her picture taken with one of them. For eternity.

JILL: Trevor's not so bad.

BETHANY: He spit in my beef stew.

JILL: That was freshman year! Way to hold a grudge.

CHELSEA: It's one thing to do it privately. Take him aside and say, "Hey, Aaron. Want to go to prom?" And then he'll say, "No, because I'm a horrible human being and I can't see that you, Jenna, are amazing." Then at least she has some dignity.

BETHANY: She thinks a big ordeal will surprise him into saying yes. She thinks it'll be fun.

JILL: Public humiliation. Super fun.

CHELSEA: I mean, the corsage industry alone...

JILL: What?

CHELSEA: Consumerism. The corsage industry alone...

JILL: You are going to ace your AP tests.

CHELSEA: You think so?

JILL: Absolutely. *(Snatches the Doritos back.)*

BETHANY: Who knows? Maybe he'll say yes. Maybe Jenna will have a great time, and a great story to tell her grandkids about the time she went to prom with the first chair trumpet player who had perfect hair. It's romantic.

JILL: His hair's not that great. He uses more product than I do.

CHELSEA: What she should do is, she should do an anti-promposal. Make a big sign in the cafeteria that says, "Nobody go to prom with me because it's a joke!"

BETHANY: She wants to go to prom. You can't save people from themselves.

(JENNA enters with a sign, shell-shocked.)

Jenna! Are you okay?

JILL: Did you do it? Oh, no. It tanked, didn't it? He said no, didn't he?

JENNA: I was in the art room. Working on my sign. See? I made the word "prom" too big so the "with me" is kinda squished.

(She holds up the sign. It reads, "Aaron, will you go to prom with me?" as advertised.)

BETHANY: Sure.

JILL: Handwriting is hard. I blame technology.

CHELSEA: Wait, I thought you were going with, "You plus me equals prom"?

JILL: No, that was when she was going to surprise him outside the math lab.

BETHANY: Let her finish her story.

CHELSEA: Sorry. I'm caught up.

JENNA: So I was trying to fix it, you know? This "with me" part. When I heard this noise in the hall. A trumpet.

(The others exchange dark glances.)

He did a whole thing for her. He played her a song. There were flowers. I think there was a monkey, but I might have been hallucinating.

BETHANY: Who'd he ask?

JENNA: Athena Williams.

JILL: Of course he did.

BETHANY: And she said yes?

JILL: Of course she did. Ugh. I can't wait to go to college.

CHELSEA: When I go to college, I'm going to study anthropology, and then I'm going to come back to high school and, like, observe everything.

JILL: You do that now.

CHELSEA: Yeah, but I'll be in college. So I can observe from afar. And get credit for it.

BETHANY: I'm sorry, Jenna. *(Hugs her.)*

JENNA: What am I gonna do with all this puffy paint?

BETHANY: If there's one thing high school has taught me, it's there's always another opportunity for puffy paint.

JILL: Know what I say? Bullet dodged. That guy's a jerk and he doesn't deserve your puffy paint.

CHELSEA: Things about college that are awesome: No prom. No Aaron Scott. No curfew. Just me, total freedom, living a life of the mind.

JILL: Did you just say, "Life of the mind"?

CHELSEA: Yes, and I regret nothing. *(Snatches the Doritos back.)*

JENNA: But that's just it! High school's going to be over in two months. This is our last chance. And maybe prom is stupid, but I want to do all the stuff people do in high school. I don't want to skip stuff. I want to go to prom.

CHELSEA: The boys in this school are mouth-breathing trolls.

JENNA: So?

CHELSEA: So, if you want to do something, and you have to rely on mouth-breathing trolls to do it...you see? It's a no-win situation. It's garbage.

JENNA: So what's our option? Not go to prom?

CHELSEA: Who needs it? I'm going to binge-watch horror movies and eat popcorn.

BETHANY: I guess I should stay home and study.

JILL: Wow.

BETHANY: What?

JILL: I thought Chelsea's thing was depressing.

BETHANY: It's not depressing! I like studying.

CHELSEA: Well, at least none of us have dates. We're all in it together. Right?

BETHANY: Right.

(Jill is conspicuously silent.)

CHELSEA: Jill?

JILL: Hmm?

CHELSEA: Are you going to prom?

JILL: Perhaps.

CHELSEA: Did you not hear what I said about the fascist garbage?

JILL: Yeah, I know. But Trevor asked me and I just thought—

CHELSEA: Trevor?! From low brass?!

BETHANY: Jill! He spit in my stew!

JILL: Okay, true confession: I kinda thought that was funny.

CHELSEA: I can't believe this. You of all people.

JILL: Prom is garbage, but sometimes it's fun to do garbage things. There. I said it.

JENNA: See? Even Jill is going. Jill, you guys. If Jill can go, I can go. I am going to prom.

CHELSEA: You don't have a date.

JENNA: Yes, I do.

CHELSEA: With who?

JENNA: With Bethany.

BETHANY: Excuse me?

JENNA: Who better? Who is always neat and organized and on time? Bethany. Who gives really thoughtful birthday gifts?

JILL & CHELSEA: Bethany.

JENNA: Who actually cares about me and appreciates me? Who's the sweetest person I know?

BETHANY: Aw! Thanks, Jenna!

JILL: No, this is a bad plan. You should go with Chelsea. Chelsea's fun.

BETHANY: Hey, I'm fun!

CHELSEA: No, Jill's right. I'm way funner. It's the water balloon theory. How likely is someone to throw water balloons? That's how fun they are. Bethany, you're like three percent likely. I'm like eighty-eight percent.

BETHANY: There's gonna be water balloons at prom? I don't know if I'm prepared.

CHELSEA: Bethany, how many times I gotta tell you: you can't predict high-jinks.

BETHANY: Jenna, you should go with me, and we'll throw water balloons at Chelsea.

CHELSEA: Don't water-balloon the messenger, Bethany.

JENNA: No, here's what I'm gonna do. I'm going to prom with Bethany and Chelsea. A prom that is both sweet and fun. That's the perfect prom. Will you go with me?

BETHANY: That is so sweet! Yes!

JENNA: You too, Chelsea. You're going.

CHELSEA: Nope.

JILL: Come on! Subvert the system already!

CHELSEA: This isn't a promposal, it's a prom dictatorship. If I'm going to prom, I expect to be asked. With puffy paint, thank you.

JENNA: Fine. *(Kneels down, crosses out "Aaron" on her sign and replaces it with "C and B.")* C and B, will you go to prom with me?

BETHANY: Neat, it rhymes!

CHELSEA: I grudgingly accept.

BETHANY: Yay!! This'll be so fun, you guys! Poor Jill's stuck with Trevor.

JILL: Don't judge me, but I think he's kinda cute.

CHELSEA: *(Sighs.)* You can't save people from themselves. At least we're together. Clarinets Forever!

JILL, BETHANY & JENNA: Clarinets Forever!

(*The end.*)

The Author Speaks

What inspired you to write this play?

We didn't have elaborate promposals when I was in high school, but we sure did have a lot of conflicting feelings about prom. Do you have to have a date? Must it be from the opposite sex? If you go with a friend, are you admitting defeat of some kind? Is it better to go, or not go? Is it truly fun, or just a rite of passage, or both?

Have you dealt with the same theme in other works that you have written?

This is my first time tackling prom, but I love to write about women and girls trying to navigate their way through a culture that doesn't always make it easy on them.

What do you hope to achieve with this work?

I hope four actors have a total blast, dismantling the patriarchy while also sometimes partying with it. I hope this play gives voice to the idea that things are complicated and there aren't always "right" answers to questions like, "Is prom worth the aggravation?"

What are the most common mistakes that occur in productions of your work?

Sometimes actors get too aware of the comedy at the expense of the realism. Just deliver the lines honestly, and the jokes will take care of themselves.

How did you research the subject?

I was a teen girl in an American high school, and our clarinet section was all girls, and all hilarious.

Shakespeare gave advice to the players in *Hamlet*; if you could give advice to your cast what would it be?

Learn your lines early, so you can stop worrying about it and start having fun on stage.

About the Author

Megan Gogerty is a playwright and solo performer. Her play *Bad Panda* (Theatre Without Borders, Beijing; Iron Crow Theatre Co.; WordBRIDGE Boomerang Playwright honoree; Syzygy Theatre/LA Writers Center series) was published by Original Works Publishing. Megan's musical drama *Love Jerry* was produced in the New York Musical Theatre Festival where it won multiple awards including three Talkin' Broadway Citations and four NYMF Excellence Awards including Excellence in Writing (Book). Her ten-minute play *Rumple Schmumple* (Dramatic Pub.) was a Kennedy Center/National ACTF honoree. Other plays include *Aberzombie* (published by YouthPLAYS), *Housebroken, My Beautiful Deadbeat Dad,* and *Feet First In The Water With A Baby In My Teeth.* Her musical tribute album to the TV show *Buffy the Vampire Slayer* is widely available online. Megan was a Playwrights' Center Jerome Fellow, a WordBRIDGE alum, and she earned her MFA in Playwriting from the University of Texas at Austin. She currently teaches playwriting at the University of Iowa.

About YouthPLAYS

YouthPLAYS (www.youthplays.com) is a publisher of award-winning professional dramatists and talented new discoveries, each with an original theatrical voice, and all dedicated to expanding the vocabulary of theatre for young actors and audiences. On our website you'll find one-act and full-length plays and musicals for teen and pre-teen (and even college) actors, as well as duets and monologues for competition. Many of our authors' works have been widely produced at high schools and middle schools, youth theatres and other TYA companies, both amateur and professional, as well as at elementary schools, camps, churches and other institutions serving young audiences and/or actors worldwide. Most are intended for performance by young people, while some are intended for adult actors performing for young audiences.

YouthPLAYS was co-founded by professional playwrights Jonathan Dorf and Ed Shockley. It began merely as an additional outlet to market their own works, which included a substantial body of award-winning published and unpublished plays and musicals. Those interested in·their published plays were directed to the respective publishers' websites, and unpublished plays were made available in electronic form. But when they saw the desperate need for material for young actors and audiences—coupled with their experience that numerous quality plays for young people weren't finding a home—they made the decision to represent the work of other playwrights as well. Dozens and dozens of authors are now members of the YouthPLAYS family, with scripts available both electronically and in traditional acting editions. We continue to grow as we look for exciting and challenging plays and musicals for young actors and audiences.

About ProduceaPlay.com

Let's put up a play! Great idea! But producing a play takes time, energy and knowledge. While finding the necessary time and energy is up to you, ProduceaPlay.com is a website designed to assist you with that third element: knowledge.

Created by YouthPLAYS' co-founders, Jonathan Dorf and Ed Shockley, ProduceaPlay.com serves as a resource for producers at all levels as it addresses the many facets of production. As Dorf and Shockley speak from their years of experience (as playwrights, producers, directors and more), they are joined by a group of award-winning theatre professionals and experienced teachers from the world of academic theatre, all making their expertise available for free in the hope of helping this and future generations of producers, whether it's at the school or university level, or in community or professional theatres.

The site is organized into a series of major topics, each of which has its own page that delves into the subject in detail, offering suggestions and links for further information. For example, Publicity covers everything from Publicizing Auditions to How to Use Social Media to Posters to whether it's worth hiring a publicist. Casting details Where to Find the Actors, How to Evaluate a Resume, Callbacks and even Dealing with Problem Actors. You'll find guidance on your Production Timeline, The Theater Space, Picking a Play, Budget, Contracts, Rehearsing the Play, The Program, House Management, Backstage, and many other important subjects.

The site is constantly under construction, so visit often for the latest insights on play producing, and let it help make your play production dreams a reality.

More from YouthPLAYS

Aesop Refabled by Nicole B. Adkins, Jeff Goode, Adam Hahn, Samantha Macher, Liz Shannon Miller, Dominic Mishler, Mike Rothschild and Dave Ulrich
Comedy. 45-60 minutes. 3-11 males, 3-11 females (3-21 performers possible).

One of L.A.'s edgiest theatre companies brings a modern spin to Aesop's classic yarns, as eight timeless fables get a 21st century reboot. Cupcake bullies, tween warriors, scheming cheerleaders and apocalyptic yellow butterfly people... Each tale takes an unexpected twist in this innovative offering!

Herby Alice Counts Down to Yesterday by Nicole B. Adkins
Comedy. 30-35 minutes. 3 females, 3 males, 4-20+ either (10-50+ performers possible).

Middle school rocket scientist Herby Alice has ambitions as big as the universe, and no time for interviews. Rose Plum, media hopeful, needs a juicy story to get in good with the school broadcast elite. How far is she willing to go to be a star? Or will mad scientists, aliens, befuddled teachers, demanding executives, and the space-time continuum overrun the show?

An Avalanche of Murder by Matt Buchanan
Comic Mystery. 75-85 minutes. 8-12 females, 4-7 males (13-16 performers possible).

In this affectionate spoof of old-fashioned murder mysteries, the Hopkins family is trapped in a house by a freak avalanche, and they're dropping like flies. It's up to young Mary and Anthony to figure out who's killing them off one by one—and bragging about it on a dead phone—before there's nobody left.

HKFN: The Abbreviated Adventures of Huckleberry Finn
by Jeff Goode
Comedy. 25-35 minutes. 3-8 females, 2-6 males (5-10 performers possible).

The actor playing Huck runs away from a production of Twain's controversial classic, **The Adventures of Huckleberry Finn**. But when the actor who plays Jim runs away too and troublemakers Duke & King join in, their fugitive theatre company launches into a series of misadventures—while the domineering Aunt Polly tries to force them back into the "real" play. In the chaos, that play—and its discussion about race—may be happening without them knowing it.

Caliban's Island by Diana Burbano
Dramedy. 50-60 minutes. 2 females, 2 males, 1 either.

Characters from Shakespeare's **Twelfth Night** and **The Tempest** intertwine as a pair of twins are shipwrecked on an island, encountering a half-human "monster," fairies and a young girl with magical powers who has been there since babyhood. Mortals will struggle with the magical; loyalty will wrestle with love, and wishes, dreams, and wisdom will collide, leaving no one unchanged.

Dear Chuck by Jonathan Dorf
Dramedy. 30-40 minutes. 8-30+ performers (gender flexible).

Teenagers are caught in the middle—they're not quite adults, but they're definitely no longer children. Through scenes and monologues, we meet an eclectic group of teens trying to communicate with that wannabe special someone, coping with a classmate's suicide, battling controlling parents, swimming for that island of calm in the stormy sea of technology—and many others. What they all have in common is the search for their "Chuck," that elusive moment of knowing who you are. Also available in a full-length version.

Scareville by Julia Edwards

Comedy for Young Audiences with Music. 40-50 minutes. 3+ females, 2+ males (5+ gender-flexible performers possible).

Milo and Clare are afraid...of lots of things. And there's good reason when they find themselves trapped in Scareville one dark, haunted night, surrounded by six-foot spiders, zombies and Dr. Fear himself. Will they end up being eaten by Sally the Black Widow? Or will Mike the Zombie's lesson on brains teach them a thing or two about fear?

Robin Hood and the Heroes of Sherwood Forest by Randy Wyatt

Adventure. 60-70 minutes. 9-30 males, 6-24 females (18-40+ performers possible).

This fresh adaptation of the classic English tale emphasizes a community of heroes as Robin Hood and his friends band together to save the people of Nottingham from unjust taxation and poverty at the hands of Prince John and his longsuffering yet cruel Sheriff. Two gypsy orphans, Maid Marion's handmaiden and a mysterious stranger share a secret that could win the day—or see Robin hanged by morning!

Les Examables by Don Zolidis

Comedy. 100-110 minutes. 8-28 females, 5-25 males (15-40+ performers possible).

Tired of too much standardized testing in her high school, high achiever Anna Ullman stages a protest and finds herself made principal. But ultimate power comes with its own problems (especially after death threats from the all-powerful State Board of Ed), and soon Anna descends into madness, imposing even more standardized testing. It's up to her ex-best friend, Lola, to bring down this new tyrant. Soon Lola is manning barricades and singing triumphantly awesome songs in this satire based on the mega-musical *Les Misérables*.

Made in the USA
Columbia, SC
22 February 2022